Channels
& Tunnels

Channels & Tunnels

Reflections on Britain and Abroad

Nicholas Henderson

WEIDENFELD AND NICOLSON
LONDON

Copyright © by Sir Nicholas Henderson 1987

All rights reserved. No part of this publication may be reproduced, stored in a retrieval system, or transmitted, in any form or by any means, electronic, mechanical, photocopying, recording or otherwise, without the prior permission of the copyright holder.

First published in Great Britain by
George Weidenfeld & Nicolson Limited
91 Clapham High Street
London SW4 7TA

ISBN 0 297 79076 5

Printed and bound in Great Britain by
Butler & Tanner Limited
Frome and London

Contents

Introduction	1
The Tunnel	5
Different Approaches to Foreign Policy	65
America and the Falklands	83
Britain's Economic Performance since 1979; and Relations with the European Community	109
Britain's Decline: its Causes and Consequences	141
Index	159

Introduction

Britain's link with the outside world is the connecting thread of these five pieces. The pattern is formed by the impact made on me personally by the people and events encountered over the past fifteen years when I served as British Ambassador in Poland, West Germany, France and the United States and subsequently on my return to Britain. In the process of watching and negotiating, certain shapes have formed in the mind's eye, and a number of conclusions have become inescapable – about government, about relations between countries, and about the divide between the official and unofficial worlds.

The first article is a personal account of the proceedings from mid-1984 to 20 January 1986 when the British and French Governments awarded the mandate for the building of a fixed Channel link to the joint consortium of the Channel Tunnel Group and France Manche. I was chairman of the Channel Tunnel Group for much of this time; and it may well be asked what on earth I was doing *'dans cette galère'*, a question, to be sure, that I was frequently putting to myself during the protracted negotiations. I explain in the text how I came to take on this task after my retirement from the Diplomatic Service.

I should make it clear that I am not providing a detailed description of our project. It is not a history of Channel-link ideas since the time of Napoleon Bonaparte. Nor is it even a full record of the short time-span covered. Few details are given, for instance, of what was happening on the French side; nor am I able to provide a comprehensive chronicle of what was going on in governmental circles in London. It is an entirely personal view of the features that I best remember, illustrating as they do to me the contrast between the still surface of public events and the rough waters beneath, the varying methods of business and government, and the sort of issues, some searing, others life-enhancing, that arise in any negotiation involving two countries as set in their different ways as France and Britain. Despite these qualifications, immodesty forbids my saying that I think I may have got it wrong.

None of the participants in our project bears any responsibility for what I have written, which, as I have said, is merely my own individual tale.

The second piece is the text of a lecture I gave to the Department of War Studies, King's College, London, in the spring of 1986. My subject, 'Different Approaches to Foreign Policy,' describes the divergent ways the three countries in which I have most recently lived, the Federal Republic of Germany, France and the United States, see the outside world, distinctions that arise from a variety of causes including geographical situation and contrasted histories. At the beginning of the year I had given a similar lecture in Oxford, the Romanes Lecture, but I am publishing the one to King's College, London, because it is more up to date.

The third report, on America and the Falklands, has been published previously in *The Economist*. It tells the story, as I saw it from the Embassy in Washington, of securing US support for the British side in the Falklands War. Apart from the inherent interest of a complicated negotiation of this kind against the background of war and the peculiar problems and opportunities facing a foreign diplomat in Washington, my main motive for writing this account was to put on record the enormous help the United States gave us over the Falklands War. I ran into opposition in Whitehall when I said I wanted to write on this subject, as did *The Economist*, which was eager to publish my account. The reasons for this hostility have never been clear to me. But I believe that the Ministry of Defence saw difficulties in what I might say about weapons and communications, and, by implication, about anything that might suggest that our own military effort was not entirely self-reliant. I was also told that the State Department feared that publication would revive the feelings of resentment aroused in Latin America at the time of the war by the support given to us by the US Government. But the United States Secretary of Defense, Caspar Weinberger, with whom I was in correspondence on the subject, was keen that the record should be made public. He provided me with detailed information about the military supplies made available to us at short notice in the war.* This and other material was drawn upon by Simon Jenkins in a subsequent article, published in *The Economist* on 3 March 1984, which gave a full account of the military backing we had received from the United States. In paying tribute now to the pertinacity of *The Economist* in fighting the battle for publication I should also like to thank that paper's editor for agreeing to republication of the article here.

Finally, I have tried to assess Britain's economic performance since Mrs Thatcher's Government came to power in May 1979, compared with the achievements of France and Germany over the same period; and to give a brief account of how we are now judged by our partners as members of the European Community. This is a follow-up to the confidential Valedictory Despatch I wrote from Paris on retirement from the Foreign Service, the text of which *The Economist* pirated and published in 1979, and which is now reproduced here legally. The published despatch was headed 'Britain's Decline: its Causes and Consequences.' It received a great deal of publicity, partly because it was forbidden fruit. The notoriety it achieved reminded me of Khrushchev's remark about how well the tsars understood their people.

---

*On 6 November 1986, long after this book was completed, *The Times* published an article by Sir John Nott, the British Secretary of State for Defence at the time of the Falklands War, comparing our success then with the fiasco of Suez. He paid tribute to Mr Weinberger personally and to the USA in general for the support they gave us over the Falklands.

Introduction

Seeing that the Russian peasants refused to eat potatoes, one tsar fenced in the potato fields, with the result that the peasants climbed over the obstructions and stole what they had previously rejected, thereafter greatly enjoying the taste.

It is striking how much vitality the topic of decline generates. A remarkable book by Martin Wiener, entitled *English Culture and the Decline of the Industrial Spirit 1850–1980*, begins as follows:

> The leading problem of modern British history is the explanation of economic decline. It has not always been thus. Until the later nineteen-sixties the generally accepted frame for the history of Britain over the previous century was that of a series of success stories: the bloodless establishment of democracy, the evolution of the welfare state, triumph in two world wars, and the enlightened relinquishment of empire. Such a happy frame, however, became increasingly hard to maintain as, having steered clear of the rocks of political turmoil or military defeat, the British found themselves becalmed in an economic Sargasso sea.

Why we find ourselves in this Sargasso sea seems to excite as much enduring interest as the sinking of the *Titanic*. Besides, the meaning of 'decline' is disputable; but that is not, I think, true of the statistics I have used, I am grateful to several souces for help over these: the Central Statistical Office, the Department of Employment, the Department of Trade and Industry, the Department of Education and Science, the Organization for Economic Co-operation and Development (OECD) and Imperial Chemical Industries (ICI).

For the assessment I now make I have relied largely on the opinions of people with whom I have discussed the subject in person; their names are given on pp. 111–13.

I am grateful to all those who have taken the trouble to give me their views. The use to which I have put them is my responsibility alone.

I must conclude by saying that I have no axe to grind beyond the wish to see the restoration of Britain's economic vitality, and its integration into a European framework which can become an independent influence and force in the world. Unless we belong to such a structure, and participate fully it in, I do not think that this country will be able in the future to provide the opportunities which will enable its people to develop and fulfil their particular talents and aspirations.

Finally, I must thank Mrs Mary Cozens for all the work she has done on this book, with the acquiescence of my colleagues at Hambros and with the help of their word processor, a development that surely must rank not far behind the invention of printing in the annals of authors' blessings.

August 1986

THE TUNNEL

Relaunching the Link

This precious stone set in the silver sea,
Which serves it in the office of a wall,
Or as a moat defensive to a house,
Against the envy of less happier lands,

John of Gaunt hovered over all our negotiations, endorsing the hunch of many who feared that we were undermining the Channel moat, seen as a wall defensive for these islands against infection and the hand of war. This public scepticism, mounting in some people to anxiety, was the first and not the least enduring of the problems we had to deal with. But of course it was not a difficulty for our proposal alone: doubts about the principle of any link were directed at all those who submitted projects. What all the competitors therefore had to face from the start was a battle on two fronts: against those who were opposed to a fixed link of any kind; and against each other in a bid to secure the mandate from the French and British Governments.

Given the historic fears that we would be treading on a national nerve, and allowing for the apathy that nowadays stultifies any attempt to do anything new, I must say, looking back, how surprised I am by the Prime Minister's categorical statement in November 1984 in favour of a link. It was a turning point. After meeting the French President that day she declared her support for the idea of a link, provided it could be built by private enterprise and without money or financial guarantees from government.

In the past the French have always wanted a link. It has been the British who have been obstructive: throughout the last century and until two decades ago they held back for security reasons; more recently, in 1975, from reluctance to spend government money for building a tunnel when the British people had so little enthusiasm for Europe. However, by the time the project was revived in 1984, security fears were no longer valid and it was accepted by all those considering a scheme that it would have to be financed privately. Mrs Thatcher did not simply make a matter-of-fact statement of support on 30 November 1984; she enthused, exclaiming that 'it really would be something very exciting ... a project which can show visibly how the technology of this age has moved to link the Continent and Britain closer together'.

The Prime Minister's decision had two main impulses: the desire to encourage some major industrial enterprise such as Britain had not carried out since the Second World War and one which would provide a good deal of employment; and the wish to make some positive move towards our European Community partners, with whom we had been wrangling for so long over the Community budget. Months later those close to the Prime Minister continued to be surprised by her decision to commit herself so wholeheartedly to the project.

Once the two Governments had decided in favour of a fixed link, it might have been thought that that would have settled the principle and that the task of those who sought to win the contract would have been limited to persuading the two Governments that theirs was the best project. But it did not work out like that. We always had to take account of public and parliamentary opinion. We had to understand and meet the instinctive resistance of an island people[1] to a fixed Channel link, as well as the opposition of particular groups, for example the environmentalists and those living in Kent, who believed that we were despoiling the Garden of England. The antagonism to any link was always strong.

The Prime Minister made another statement on the day of the joint summit meeting which was to cause our Channel Tunnel Group (CTG) recurring trouble in the months ahead. Drawing attention to the need to consider all types of link, she said to the BBC, 'many people have a great dream that they would like to get in their car at Dover and drive all the way through to Calais. So we must consider that possibility too.' This remark reinforced the surmise of many that the Prime Minister favoured a drive-through, just as it plagued our group in our effort to explain to the public that, within the limits of current technology, such a project was not now feasible.

The Channel Tunnel Group,[2] an amalgam of construction contractors and banks, had been put together in 1984, its main purpose being to revitalize the idea of a tunnel link. Its members had examined all manner of schemes including a drive-through. They took account of the findings of the 1981 Report of the House of Commons Select Committee for Transport, which had examined ten schemes for a privately financed link; also the Report of the Anglo-French Study Group,[3] an official enquiry into the technical and economic aspects of a link; and the Report of the Anglo-French Financing Group, a study comprising leading banks in the two countries.

They concluded, in accordance with the findings of each of these reports, that the only scheme that was technically and financially feasible in the

---

[1] Shakespeare has encouraged exaggeration about our island story. The sea has not always provided protection from invasion, as the ethnic mixture of our population attests. We only became a maritime power in the middle of the sixteenth century, so, keeping within historical perspective, we should now be able to see that the tunnel will not be breaching any time-honoured invulnerability, crucial though the sea-wall was to defence at certain moments – moments which preceded the development of modern weapons.

[2] See p. 64 for the composition of the Group and representation on the Channel Tunnel Group Board.

[3] Command 8561, June 1982.

foreseeable future was a tunnel. This would take through-trains and a shuttle, a kind of 'rolling-road', that would carry vehicles of all kinds at frequent intervals, taking half an hour for the journey. It is true that originally the Anglo-French Financing Group believed that such a link could only be constructed with government, or government-backed, money; but this view was modified when the bankers became more optimistic about the length of construction-time and revenue prospects. What the Channel Tunnel Group were waiting for was some spark to ignite the idea and to bring it into the realm of practical politics; the joint statement of the two Heads of Government of 30 November had done precisely this.

But to revert a little in time, I first became involved with the promotion of the scheme early in 1984. This arose out of my membership of the Board of Tarmac, one of the construction companies participating in the Channel Tunnel Group. But it also reflected my personal commitment to the idea of a link that had burned within me since the cancellation of the previous project a decade earlier, just before I went to our Embassy in Paris: a new connexion between Britain and the European Continent that I believed would have both practical and symbolic significance.

In the middle of 1984 I arranged a dinner for the members of the Board to meet Peter Rees, the Financial Secretary at the Treasury. It may seem eccentric in retrospect that this, our first collective meeting with a member of the Government, should have taken place with a Minister in the Treasury; but our purpose was to find out whether there was any give in the intentions of the Government as regards financial support. We also hoped to test the degree of keenness in ministerial circles for the idea of a fixed link at all. It was evident that Rees was surprised that we had fastened upon him; as he told us politely but firmly, as member of Parliament for Dover he could not possibly be regarded as an advocate of a fixed link, which would be taken by many of his constituents as a serious threat to local employment. He also made it quite clear that there would be no government money or financial support.

Our next ministerial sortie was to Nicholas Ridley, the Secretary of State for Transport, whom we saw in July. In retrospect, I regard this meeting as the essential prologue to our project. It was the first detailed discussion that members of our group had with a Minister and his officials. Not that Ridley was encouraging. No doubt his officials, who sat inscrutably at the table, had reminded him beforehand that they had been there before and had experienced the disillusionment of the 1975 cancellation. The line Ridley took with us was that he was waiting for prospective promoters to come forward. So far there was just Euroroute (see p. 10) and us. Government prejudice was probably in favour of a drive-through scheme; but it was up to promoters to persuade Ministers that their own scheme was the most attractive and the most easily financed. However, he wished to make it absolutely clear that nobody could expect anything from the government in terms of financial support. It was impossible to come away from the meeting with any sense of euphoria, but the ball was in our court and we were determined to keep it in play. I wrote to Ridley in October 1984 telling him of an important change that we had made in our scheme since our meeting in mid-summer. The construction period had been reduced from six years to four and a half, which should greatly help the financing. Moreover, by now there had been the important shift that I have already mentioned in the prognosis about the chances of financing the project from the market without government backing. From what we gathered, the Secretary of State himself remained very cautious. His officials told us in mid-September that he was neutral about the idea of a fixed link of any kind. He was not pro or anti, and certainly was not in favour of any particular scheme. All the same, if a credible project emerged, a Conservative Government would not stand in its way.

Between that time and the November announcement by President Mitterrand and Mrs Thatcher a certain amount of ministerial activity took place in Whitehall, stimulated, I suspect, by awareness of the promoters' persistence and of the likely availabiliy to them of private finance. In September–October British Ministers took the decision in principle to back a scheme on this basis. Incidentally the fact that Ministers only reached this decision in the autumn of 1984 renders nugatory the charge later made by James Sherwood that when he bought the ferry company Sealink in July of that year the Government had already decided on a fixed link. He knew in July, as did everyone, that a fixed link was a possibility, but he is as wrong to slur over this in retrospect as he is to say that a decision had in fact been taken by then. In the middle of November Ridley met Paul Quilès, the French Minister of Town Planning, Housing and Transport, and Jean Auroux, the French Minister of Transport, in Paris; they decided to put officials to work in both countries to draw up guidelines to be followed by any would-be promoters. The French, at this stage, I believe, would have preferred to leave open the possibility that government money might be available for the project (particularly European Community support), but in the face of adamant opposition from the British the idea was dropped. It was agreed, upon President Mitterrand's initiative, that the announcement of the Anglo-French decision would be made by himself and Mrs Thatcher when they met at the end of the month. He was eager to stamp it with his authority. When the time came for the joint public statement everyone on both sides was surprised by the sudden enthusiasm displayed by Mrs Thatcher. This was, as I have said, a turning point.

Spurred on by the November decision, the Channel Tunnel Group went into a gallop. Their pace was matched by Euroroute, a rival scheme which was relaunched in November 1984.[4] The Euroroute project had been initiated

---

[4] Euroroute comprised: the banks Sociétés Générales and Paribas; Trafalgar House;

by Ian McGregor when he was head of British Steel; the chairman now was Sir Nigel Broackes, who was also chairman of Trafalgar House. The scheme envisaged bridges leading out from either coast, two spirals from the ends of these bridges down to the seabed, and a tube resting on the seabed as conduit for the traffic. The project was a complicated one, and indeed very expensive, but it had the attraction of providing a drive-through. It soon won important French partners. I had some difficulty in persuading my colleagues in the Channel Tunnel Group that it had to be taken seriously. They believed that Euroroute would run into all sorts of difficulties because of the obstructions it would cause in the Channel. The International Maritime Organization (IMO), which is responsible for ensuring unimpeded navigation of waterways, would have to be consulted about the Euroroute scheme. That would mean reference to over a hundred countries and would produce inevitable delay. However, when in March 1985, soon after I had been made chairman of the Channel Tunnel Group, I came to check this with the Department of Transport I was given a very different picture. The officials told me that it had been decided that IMO approval would only be needed for projects which required a change in the traffic separation scheme, by which ships keep to one or other side of the Channel, according to their direction; while projects merely affecting the in-shore zones or the separation zone (the no-man's water between the shipping lanes) would simply have to be notified to the IMO. The Euroroute scheme was not therefore likely to encounter any navigational objections. The two bridges would stand in in-shore waters; so too would the two islands, leaving the navigational channels unimpeded. The ventilation shaft for the immersed tube would be constructed in the separation zone – that is, where there could be no traffic to obstruct. True, the placing of a large tube might create hydrological problems but these should not prove insurmountable. 'The truth is,' the senior Department of Transport official told me, 'that Euroroute is a runner.' Indeed I gained the impression in these early days that in the minds of many people in the Ministry of Transport it was seen as a very promising runner.

The timetable set by the Governments after they had made their momentous decision was a tight one. The French parliamentary elections were due in March 1986, and their presidential election in 1988, which was also the latest date for a general election in Britain. Agreement between the two Governments on the project before March 1986, and the passage of any necessary legislation well before the run-up to the presidential or general election, were seen as essential if the issue was not to founder on the rocks

---

John Howard; Fairclough; Grands Travaux de Marseille; British Shipbuilders; British Steel; and Alsthom Atlantique.

of party politics in either country. But it was not just a question of avoiding pre-electoral shoals. If organizations in the two countries were going to work up momentum on such a project they could not be left hanging about indefinitely without a decision by the two Governments; likewise, if the whole idea of a link was put off indefinitely the groups now gathering together and devoting time and money to it would lose heart. It was a widely held view at this stage that, if the opportunity that seemed to be available for the taking between 1984 and 1986 was not seized upon, a resumption of interest in a fixed link would be unlikely before the end of this century at the earliest.

The first deadline of the two Governments was one they imposed upon themselves, as an earnest of their sense of urgency – an undertaking to issue their guidelines by the spring of 1985. I believe it was the French who, aware of the British tendency to procrastinate, suggested the tight timetable. A few points of reference, of the kind which British officials know that their Ministers need if they are not to feel they have embarked upon a dangerous course, had been set down in Whitehall before decisions had been taken; but no thorough work had been done on the guidelines and no machinery had been established for Anglo-French collaboration in drawing them up. The first time officials from both sides met for this purpose was in the second week of January 1985. The British side was led by Andrew Lyall, Under-Secretary at the Department of Transport, the French by Raoul Rudeau. By the time the two teams got together there was less than two months in which to meet the deadline. This time-pressure led to the establishment in Whitehall of a remarkably effective organization for tackling the wide-ranging problems, a system which forestalled inter-departmental wrangles and continued as the main motor for moving the British side along together until the mandate was awarded in January 1986.

The main problem for the CTG at the end of 1984 and in the first months of 1985 was to find a French partner. There were plenty of bilateral contacts between contractors and banks, and there were many on the French side who agreed with our general ideas for a link, but there was nothing on the other side of the Channel comparable to our organization and nothing therefore with which we could form a joint consortium. Yet that was essential if we were to produce a scheme acceptable to the French Government.

I myself went to Paris in December 1984 to pursue this search. Accompanied by Tony Gueterbock, who had been one of the pioneers of the project and knew the whole gamut of the tunnel from rabies to cost overruns, I called on the French Minister of Transport, Jean Auroux. I also saw representatives of banks and contractors. It was the first time I had conducted business in Paris since ceasing to be Ambassador there in 1979; and I found my role as private negotiator very different from that of Ambassador. Far from arriving in a Rolls-Royce, I travelled by Metro, a means of transport which Tony Gueterbock thought would be good for my image with the socialist Government, as well as quicker. However, this brainwave did not seduce the French Minister, particularly as we lost our way and arrived late at his office. However, he had laid on a breakfast party for us and was most amicable. Auroux's main interest seemed to be to find out whether the Train de Grande Vitesse (TGV) was going to be allowed to come to London. Throughout the negotiations the TGV was often brandished before us by the French like some talisman, whereas to British Rail it was a red rag. However, Auroux did say very clearly that he was confident that there would be a French team in place with which we could join as partner by the end of January 1985.

During this visit to Paris I also made contact with the British Embassy, although I sensed that my presence there could be awkward if anyone were to infer from it that I was receiving preferential treatment. I was determined therefore to be extremely prudent; and in fact I never sought nor received any favour. But I did derive frequent benefit from the Counsellor, Kate Timms, whose parent department was the Ministry of Agriculture. She seemed to have no difficulty taking in her stride the problems both of the tunnel and of farm prices.

Although the Prime Minister had clearly set her course for the Channel and there was no doubt about Whitehall's eagerness to spread canvas in the wake of that momentous decision, I remained anxious to find out for myself what she really felt. The chance offered when my wife and I were invited to a lunch party at Chequers on Boxing Day 1984. There were other guests but Mrs Thatcher took me aside, saying that she wanted a word, which was exactly what I wanted. But our topics were different. She was impatient to talk about Star Wars following her recent visit to Washington and her meeting with the President; or rather, it was not so much that she wanted to talk about it as to let off steam. Naturally I was receptive, but when I judged that sufficient pressure had been released I said: 'Changing the subject, Prime Minister, there is something I wish to learn from you. Are you really interested in the idea of a fixed Channel link?' I added that I was involved and I explained in what way. She said that she definitely believed in it strongly; but she preferred a drive-through. I realized that her attention was not really engaged on the subject and that she wanted to get back to Star Wars. But what she had said and the enthusiastic manner in which she had spoken was enough for me.

A few weeks later, after we had had several discursive meetings of the Channel Tunnel Group Board under rotating chairmen, the directors of the Group asked me if I would become chairman. I at first said no. I thought they needed someone with direct experience of industry. The task of putting a scheme and an organization together which would win the confidence of governments was a demanding one; it would be almost a full-time occupation and would require great drive. While declining the offer I said that I would always be ready to help, because I believed in the idea. However, subsequently I was subjected to considerable pressure and, without too much hesitation, I changed my mind and agreed to take the chairmanship on, but on the understanding that my tenure would be temporary, say for a year. I was influenced by the conviction that the Prime Minister was an enthusiastic supporter of a link; the fact that she seemed to favour a drive-through did not matter to me because she had obviously not then applied herself to the problems involved. But it made all the difference to me that she was in favour of a link in principle, because so long as she felt like that other Ministers would go along with her, whatever their inner doubts. The Foreign Secretary, for instance, had made no bones to me about his indifference to the idea. As the months went by, I did not conclude that he necessarily became converted but he certainly avoided any opposing tactics. Indeed, once the Prime Minister had given the lead I found that most Ministers fell into line on the subject. So too did the officials; I am sure that the harmony and drive in Whitehall right through to the end owed a lot to the certainty that the Prime Minister had given her backing.

Before I finally took on the chairmanship I had to consult the other companies with which I was connected, particularly Hambros, to ensure their tolerance of the priority calls on my time that the tunnel would entail. The responses were positive, reflecting I thought both generosity towards me and ignorance of the tunnel's demands. When my appointment was announced the *Financial Times* delivered a sardonic swipe under the heading 'Our Man in the Tunnel': 'given the nature of the project, one of his directorships, of reinsurance group Mercantile and General, could come in handy'.

If I am to give a fair account of how I came to take on the unaccustomed role of chairman of a still unformed consortium the prime task of which, at this stage, seemed to be to win the prize before being allowed to compete in the race, I cannot conceal the Alice in Wonderland elements that entered into it of curiosity and vanity. Seeking advice one day from Chips Keswick, the deputy chairman of Hambros Bank, about whether I should accept the post I received the firm reply that I should do no such thing – 'Nigel Broackes will eat you for breakfast,' he said. As I thought it over afterwards, this idea of Broackes's breakfast, or rather of other people's idea of Broackes's breakfast, began to rankle.

The structure and composition of the Group when I took over were sketchy. Its provisional headquarters were in Wimpey's office on the ground floor of Triangle House, Hammersmith, a building which may not deserve to survive long enough to receive a commemorative plaque, but which could always at least boast proximity to London Airport. Those working full-time at the tunnel face made up in personality what they lacked in numbers: they included Tony Gueterbock, who kept an enthusiastic eye on the whole project even when there was no enthusiasm elsewhere and who was never afraid to remind the directors that they did not know what they were talking about because, unlike him, they had not been engaged exclusively upon it for several years; Colin Stannard, seconded from the National Westminster Bank, who was in charge of finance but, despite that, never wavered in his optimism; and Don Hunt, his wife and his sizeable dog, who stood guard over public relations with the specialist help of Bill Shakespeare. Most of the people engaged were specialists seconded from their parent firms. However, at this stage we had no managing director, no project manager and no finance director – nor, as I have indicated, did we have a French partner. I found, therefore, that, whereas there were people who could advise me about important details such as ventilation, or comparable tunnels in Japan, or the requirements of the terminals, or potential equity investors, there was no one with whom I could discuss the merits of the scheme as a whole. The tendency in the organization was to rely upon the ideas of a decade ago. It was obvious to me, however, that we would have to re-examine the possibility of a drive-through tunnel; also that we would have to fashion our shuttle in such a way as to provide as good a means of movement for vehicles as a drive-through. It would not be enough to rely on 1974 technology.

A particular combination of qualities seemed to me to permeate the Channel Tunnel staff from its earliest days. They were individualists owing loyalty primarily to their parent company, yet they acknowledged a second commitment to the tunnel. Although I was unable to perceive in them much team spirit – predictably, since they were without direction – I was never in any doubt about their belief in the idea. I enjoyed dropping in on them when they were working on charts or computer runs and I always came away surer than I had been before that we would muddle through because of their talent for making the best of things.

Cliff Chetwood, Wimpey's chairman, was a regular attender at our Board meetings. The more generous he was in offers of hospitality at Triangle House, the more intense was the banter from the other directors about the amount of money he would be charging them for it. One of the features I noticed and liked about private enterprise was the absence of humbug and the emphasis on raillery whenever Good Samaritanism seemed to be getting in the way of hard-headed business. Of our directors, Frank Gibb of Taylor Woodrow and Don Holland of Balfour Beatty brought great experience to our proceedings from their involvement in the previous tunnel. From the start of our work Frank Gibb never spared himself; if at times he tended to be critical, he struck me as having a deep awareness of the frailty of human nature, and he never lost sight of the goal. Don Holland combined with the bluntness I came to associate with the construction industry an infectious good humour. Once he guffawed to me across the table after some rough and ready exchange: 'You know, Nicko, I wouldn't be surprised if you didn't write something about this one day.'

Uncompromising in opinion and language, Denis Child, deputy group chief executive of National Westminster, kept us constantly aware of what was essential if we were to get the money privately. I always knew when he was going to be particularly downright because his face would take on an unusually benign expression. Never was this more apparent than right at the end of our task when we were engaged in some last-minute negotiation with the Department of Transport and were still uncertain whether we were going to get the mandate. Denis was involved in a telephone altercation with a high official of that department. 'Do you know what an equity investment is?' he asked. I could not hear but could well imagine the indignation on the part of the high official at the other end of the line; his answer did not satisfy Denis, who went on with his cross-examination. 'Tell me, do you know what equity is?' That's torn it, I said to myself. However, I liked to think that the philosophic civil servant merely shrugged his shoulders and decided it was all part of the rough ways of private enterprise. History, however personal, must record the leading part the National Westminster Bank played in the negotiations. Midland Bank, who had participated in the Anglo-French Financing Group, joined up with us later. Nat West, however, were there throughout and never looked like faltering.

I cannot say that our Board meetings in the early days were anything but chaotic; and I am not sure that this was simply because I had had little experience of running an ill-assorted gathering of this kind. The directors did not seem to believe that their function was to proffer constructive ideas for pushing the project forward. Their tendency was to carp, as Alan Osborne of Tarmac admitted, though he himself, as I discovered, was always ready to take out a piece of paper and pencil and say how necessary it was to work things out constructively. It was difficult not to become exasperated at times by the perverse god presiding over us who seemed so slow to bless and swift to chide.

At the start of our work the contractors were at odds among themselves and there would often be shouting between them across the table. When they decided to get together before our meetings and agree upon a common line, the effect was to worry the banks and we increasingly found the two sides – the contractors and the banks – at odds. Another row flourished, this time between the clearing and the merchant banks. Bankers seem to have a way of quarrelling that strikes a note of high but clashing moral indignation; more rarefied in atmosphere but no less down to earth in substance than disputes between members of the construction industry. Eventually a *modus vivendi* was reached that Morgan Grenfell and Fleming were able to accept; Kleinwort Benson, which had hitherto been a party with them, withdrew.

Morgan Grenfell and Fleming, represented respectively by John Franklin and Christopher Moore, raised doubts about the financeability of the project; and this lack of confidence continued right up to August 1985. But, once convinced, they applied themselves unswervingly to the cause. From the early days we were under pressure from the Government – as later were our French partners from the French Government – to prevent our organization from appearing to be too dominated by the contractors. I made frequent efforts in the first months to persuade the members of the Board to admit as co-owners other organizations who were eager to join us, but the contractors would have none of it. From their point of view they believed that they had all the specialist knowledge that was required, and that by the time French partners were admitted the group of owners would be quite large enough.

Yet, if I was to sum up the overriding ethos which governed the directors and the individuals of CTG from the start until the award of the mandate, it was inarticulate faith, difficult to define or explain, but an abiding faith that we would get there in the end.

Flying to Paris at this time, I was assailed by a mixture of thoughts and feelings; and my doubts reflected the equivocal mood of public opinion. There was a wave of scepticism over whether a tunnel was required and whether one would ever be built at all. This visit to Paris served me as a timely corrective. The horrors of the journey brought home to me the desirability of what we were trying to create. It would surely be a great blessing for millions of people to avoid the lengthy time required by the airlines for checking in before the flight, the long walk to the departure gate, the queue in the proboscis before boarding, the struggle with hand luggage trying to get it into the overhead rack with other passengers pushing past in the narrow aisle, the loud, cheery but indistinct voice of the captain on the intercom wishing one a good flight, the canned music, the lack of leg room, the man in the seat in front leaning back into one's lap, the captain speaking again just as cheerily towards the end of the flight expressing the hope that one would travel again by the same airline, followed by the same hassle and queuing at the far end. Why should one have to put up with it? How could anybody be against a feasible alternative? The advantages of through-train over air travel were incontestable, I decided; the trouble was that they went too often unsung in our publicity.

By the spring of 1985 our organization was strengthened by a number of appointments. Michael Gordon, who became managing director at the end of April, had previously been managing director and chief executive of Badger, the European subsidiary of the Badger Company of Cambridge, Massachusetts.

He had recently joined Taylor Woodrow as chairman of Taylor Woodrow Management and Engineering. Those who met him invariably liked the cut of his jib, to adopt an expression I heard used of him, and he was extremely effective on television and with the press. He soon ran into criticism from the directors who, I think, resented his insistence that the ownership of our organization was wider than the sum of the contractors, whose interests were different from those of the owners as a whole – something to which the Government attached great importance. Despite criticism Gordon was never downcast. He brought a sense of order and purpose to our administration and, after all, it was under his management that the CTG won the mandate.

Melville Guest, who joined us in the early summer, had qualities that were invaluable for our Group. A seconded member of the Foreign Service, he had served with me as First Secretary at the British Embassy in Paris and had then spent five years in charge of Lucas Industries in France. So he had experience of both government and industry; he was also bilingual in French and English. At first the directors were somewhat hesitant when I said that I thought we ought to take him on; they appeared to have difficulty in believing that someone from the diplomatic world would be prepared to roll his sleeves up and be capable of doing the dirty-work on the shop floor that was necessary to put our industrial project together. Their acquiescence was eased when I told them that he was a double blue and had played rugger for Oxford University. His contribution was to prove invaluable; and I would go so far as to say that without him we would never have put together our submission in time.

Another important new addition to our team was Quentin Morris, who was taken on as financial adviser, originally upon Michael Gordon's recommendation. A former senior employee of British Petroleum, he came to us with a resounding reputation for having raised the money for the Forties Field. Friction between the merchant banks and the clearers was part of the reason for Q. Morris's appointment but we also needed someone with a brain who could put together a financial plan and sell it to potential equity investors and banks. This Q. Morris did with aplomb and without any overdue regard to susceptibilities on either side of the Channel. He was ably and unobtrusively assisted by a newcomer to our team, Ian Callaghan, who was seconded from the National Westminster Bank.

In terms of organization another important change occurred in mid-summer when we acquired as our headquarters an office at 8 Suffolk Street. Aesthetically and geographically this Nash building was an advance on Triangle House where, however, most of the staff had to continue to work. From the new Board room we could see through imposing Corinthian columns the stage door of the Haymarket Theatre. It was in Suffolk Street that we eventually signed an agreement with our French partners, who were as taken as we were by the distinction of our new address. But once again I am jumping ahead of the true sequence of events.

At the end of January 1985 Cliff Chetwood, chairman of Wimpeys, and a member of the CTG Board, had had an approach from Sir Nigel Broackes, who asked whether we would be interested in joining up with Euroroute. His idea was that he would build his road-link and we would confine the tunnels to rail traffic. We in CTG were not tempted by this offer because we did not believe in the feasibility of his road-link and because we wanted our tunnels to provide for vehicles as well as trains, for which indeed they had plenty of capacity. In rejecting Broackes's proposal Chetwood extended to Trafalgar House what he described as a 'reverse invitation' for his company to join our Group. We heard no more until Sir Nigel Broackes invited me to lunch soon after my appointment. He said that he was sure we would have to get together one day. I said that I did not think there was room for compromise. It had to be one scheme or the other. This was the first of several meetings I had with Broackes. There was never any acrimony. We never concealed anything from each other. The trouble was that there was no basis for a merger. I had great respect for Broackes's entrepreneurial skill and the considerable infrastructure behind him. I was also duly impressed by his flagship, the Trafalgar Suite at the Ritz, whence he conducted operations. When we had been awarded the mandate the following year the first telegram of congratulations I received was a personal one from Broackes.

Among the calls I made in the early weeks was one on Sir Bob Reid, chairman of British Rail. I had never entered Rail House, Euston, before and I was surprised to find that it resembled a hospital more than anything to do with railways. I had imagined that there would be illuminated charts on the walls showing the movement of freight and passenger trains, a sort of signal-box control tower. But there was nothing to suggest movement or transport of any kind near the chairman's office, where Reid and I were joined by D. P. Williams, who had experience of the previous tunnel project. Reid was most forthcoming, not surprisingly given the advantages to British Rail of a cross-Channel link. I described the kind of benefits it seemed to me BR stood to derive from long freight hauls, say from Manchester to Lyons, not to mention the prospects for passenger traffic between London and Paris when the journey would take less than three and a half hours. BR would derive nothing from the operation of the shuttle but I became quite carried away at the thought of trains whizzing to and fro from all corners of the British Isles carrying people and goods to all parts of the Continent, and I sensed that Reid shared my enthusiasm. This was particularly encouraging, on account of his reputation for being in the Prime Minister's good books.

My spirits remained moderately high after a meeting I had with John Biffen, the Leader of the House of Commons, in his room in the Palace of Westminster.

He revealed that the Government had made provision in the 1986/7 Parliamentary timetable for a Government-sponsored Hybrid Bill (a public Bill on a matter that affects private rights) providing the necessary legal authority for the project. But he also told me that the passage of such a Bill might take eight months and would be opposed by many people. I said that I assumed that if the Government sponsored it there could be no doubt about the outcome. He was not prepared to commit himself on this. I remarked that no doubt all those on both sides of the House who were anti-European would be against the Bill; to which he rejoined that hostility would not only come from those who were *anti-communautaire*. As I finished the glass of dry sherry he had given me and he drank his concoction of Cinzano, I became, as he spoke, increasingly aware of the parliamentary battle that lay ahead should we succeed in winning the mandate. Not that Biffen was negative. He was out to tell me what he knew; and he did this with an occasional guffaw of laughter that I could only suppose was merited by the comedy he saw in our enterprise.

One day at lunch in the City around this time I ran into someone whose reaction to the tunnel was a useful corrective to any euphoria.

'I see that you have taken on the tunnel,' he said in a challenging tone. 'Well, I hope you fail. I can't think of any idea I like less than that of tying ourselves up close to Europe.'

I referred to the changing pattern of British trade, of which about 50 per cent was now with the countries of the European Community, and to the surcharge that we had to endure, compared with our Community partners, on account of the heavy costs involved in crossing the Channel.

'Oh, I don't care about that', my luncheon companion replied, 'so long as we don't have all those foreigners coming out of the ground and overrunning us.' 'I am surprised you haven't mentioned rabies', I said.

'Oh, there's that too. My wife agrees with me. Why can't we be content in our own island without wishing all this trouble upon ourselves?'

I was made aware that many felt like this, even though they may have been too tactful to express it in such frank terms to my face. Some people were to say to me, with an expression which seemed to indicate how fair-minded and reasonable they thought they were, some variation of 'It would be all right if they learned English,' occasionally degenerating into 'Why can't they learn our language, damn it!'

I encountered a different type of scepticism in France around this time. The British Ambassador, Sir John Fretwell, gave a lunch party at the Embassy for me to meet André Chadeau, the head of the Société Nationale des Chemins de Fer Français (SNCF), and Bernard Thiolon, chief general manager, international, Crédit Lyonnais. Chadeau had been *préfet* of Lille a decade or so before when the British Government had cancelled the tunnel. He was therefore doubtful about *'la volonté personelle de Mrs Thatcher'*. Thiolon spoke of the tide flowing in favour of a drive-through and of the doubts in banking circles about the chances of raising money privately in the absence of some public guaranteee against the danger of cost overruns. The conviction in France that Mrs Thatcher was in favour of a drive-through was confirmed later the same day when I called on the French Prime Minister's office. These were sentiments I was to hear time and again in the months ahead on both sides of the Channel.

On a visit to Dover in March to have a look at the quarter-mile of tunnel built in the 1970s I talked with representatives of Crédit Lyonnais who had come over from France for the day for the same inspection. They spoke to me earnestly about the groundswell in France in favour of a drive-through. At the board meeting in London later that day I accordingly secured agreement from the directors that we must both re-examine the feasibility of a drive-through and be prepared to say now that we were doing so. This, I hoped, would prevent our rivals from cashing the drive-through trump. The directors were reluctant to accept the need for this; those with technical knowledge were convinced of the impracticability of a drive-through given existing technology. But they were persuaded that we must have a look at it again, so strong was public feeling about it here and in France.

In the middle of March I wrote to the chairmen of all the CTG companies describing how our organization was shaping up and what our prospects were of securing the mandate from the Governments. Towards the end of the month I prepared a memorandum for public use summarizing as follows the CTG scheme at that stage:

> The Channel Tunnel Group propose to construct twin tunnels, each of seven metres in diameter, and a smaller service tunnel. This system will provide a privately operated, roll-on roll-off shuttle to run between the British and French coasts, with trains leaving every 5 minutes, giving a capacity of 3,600 vehicles per hour in each direction. This 'rolling-road' would be operated to high standards of safety in such a way as to avoid any delay at either terminal for passengers who would, if they wished, remain in or near their vehicles for the transit. The ferry train will be brightly lit and air-conditioned. It will be operated electrically and will take less than half an hour for the transit.
>
> There will also be through rail traffic to and from all parts of the U.K. to the Continent. Passenger services between London and Paris/Brussels would be expected to take about four hours (or three hours if a high speed service were introduced in France).
>
> The Channel Tunnel Group are also examining the possibilities of a drive

through tunnel in the light of the guidelines for a fixed link issued by the British and French Governments. If there is to be an all-weather drive through scheme that would be acceptable to drivers, the only practical method would be by tunnel; the Channel Tunnel Group have studied the ideas of a bridge or immersed tube but do not consider either of these practical in terms of construction or operation.

When the Governments issued their guidelines in April 1985 our chances seemed to me to be affected by three factors. First, we had the best scheme provided we held out the prospect of a drive-through to be built if further study showed that it was technically feasible. But secondly our organization was inadequate to the task of responding to the guidelines, putting together a convincing case and convincing the Governments that we were capable of building and operating a fixed link. Third, we still had no French partner.

The Guidelines

The publication by the two Governments on 2 April 1985 of the guidelines, entitled euphemistically 'An Invitation to Promoters', was another turning point. The Governments began by describing their role, negative as regards finance, positive in respect of their political guarantee (which committed them to refrain from terminating the link during the concession period). Having listed numerous legal, security, maritime, environmental and organizational requirements, and having stipulated in a separate chapter the need for promoters to show financial 'robustness', a word that was to keep ringing in my ears like some admonition from my schooldays, the guidelines then set out the need for detailed descriptions of each project and its implications. We had thus been set a major task and one that had to be completed by 31 October. It seemed like an examination of Chinese proportions. My only solace was my awareness that the Governments had given themselves a piece of work of comparable dimensions, in that they would have to go through all our papers and choose the winner within three months of the closing date for submissions.

Introducing the guidelines to the House of Commons, Nicholas Ridley emphasized the Government's caution: 'I cannot yet tell whether a fixed link will be built across the Channel or not.' But he saw the chance ahead – for others: 'What I can say is that the private sector now has a unique opportunity.' The Labour Shadow Secretary for Transport, Mrs Gwynneth Dunwoody, responded immediately with a welcoming statement: 'We have been asking the Government for many years for precisely this sort of infrastructure development, with its impact on jobs and industry.' As if fortified by this reaction from the Opposition Front Bench, Ridley then spoke of the link as 'this exciting and imaginative project'.

By the beginning of April therefore the climate was looking more auspicious for us. But we had major tasks ahead. If the conversion of our unformulated project into a precise submission to meet the guidelines was thenceforth to be the main focus of our day-to-day work, this did not lessen the need, if we were to succeed, for keeping other features in view: we had to run the whole gamut of persuasion, public and personal; and there was still the search for the inverted Scarlet Pimpernel, a French collaborator.

Among the Ministers and members of Parliament whom I called on at this stage were Norman Tebbit, the Secretary of State for Trade and Industry, and Lord Young, Minister without Portfolio, with special responsibility in the Cabinet for employment. Tebbit thought that Euroroute carried fewer technological risks than the tunnel. Lord Young believed that our scheme would involve a trade union stranglehold; he also feared that it would favour the south-east at the expense of the north; not least important, he wanted to be able to drive through. In reply to Tebbit I told him about the years of research that had gone into our tunnel. The layer of lower chalk under the Channel was ideal for tunnelling. It struck me that Euroroute were going to have all manner of technological difficulties: the bridges, the spiral, and the immersed tube. I explained to Lord Young that under the Channel tunnel scheme there would be no question of a railway union stranglehold. The shuttle, which would take all types of vehicles, would be operated not by British Rail but by a separate organization. There would be no greater danger of union or organized stoppage than would occur on a bridge or any type of terminal. I gave an account of the proposed speed and frequency of our 'rolling road' which would get vehicles across more quickly than if they were driven across by means of any other scheme. As regards the provision of jobs and their spread throughout the British Isles, I said that there might not be much in it between us and other schemes during the construction phase. Many features of the tunnel project would be built in different parts of Britain. In the longer term the beauty of a fast rail service to the Continent was that it would greatly increase the prospects for British exports from all over the British Isles.

I also asked to see the Prime Minister, and I explained how many people in London and Paris were saying that she favoured one of the schemes, Euroroute, even though in inviting bids from promoters the Government had indicated that no decision had been reached. On 3 April *The Times* had reported that 'Mrs Thatcher's closest colleagues are already pressing for the road option.' In my letter to her asking for an interview I said that the Channel Tunnel Group were examining the possibility of a drive-through tunnel. Shortly before I called at No. 10 the Prime Minister received Laurent Fabius, the French Prime Minister. Following this meeting she had spoken with renewed enthusiasm of 'our desire to see the fixed Channel link built. It seems to be something that our generation can perform for future generations.' When I saw her on the morning of 13 May I found her looking as though she had just returned from a six-week holiday; in fact she had just had a meeting with the leaders of the Coal Board, had not been back long from a gruelling tour of South-east Asia and knew she was about to face an organized challenge to her policies from within the Conservative Party led by Francis Pym. 'Come, let's have some coffee', she said as I entered her room on the first floor overlooking the garden and the Horseguards. We met to the sound of martial music coming from a rehearsal of the Trooping of the Colour. Red uniforms moved about with precision in the background. The room has a desk at one end, china cabinets on the wall opposite the window, and chairs and a low table in front of the fireplace. Mrs Thatcher said that she did not favour any particular scheme. Nor would it be for her alone to decide which was chosen. But she did feel passionately strongly in favour of some fixed link and she believed that the decision must be taken as quickly as possible. As regards driving across, yes, she did like the idea of being able to stay in the car to reach the other side, but she realized that a drive-through might be very expensive.

I said that I would like to describe to her how the private traveller would make the crossing under our scheme. He would drive on to a new sort of conveyor, something like a rolling road; access to this would be through four different entrances, so there would be no delay in boarding. Nor would there be any delay before the conveyor departed. The transit would take about half an hour. The conveyor would be electrically operated. The traveller could remain in his car or get out into the air-conditioned and well-lit interior of the conveyor during the journey. Mrs Thatcher indicated that she now understood what we had in mind. I referred to the difficulties of driving by Euroroute; the complications of the spiral descent from a bridge over fifty yards above the sea to the tube immersed on the sea bed; the difficulties of ventilating the tube, which was to be full of vehicles emitting exhaust fumes, the possible disorientation of drivers in the tube; and the dangers of accidents.

Mrs Thatcher asked what would happen if there was a breakdown in our tunnel. I replied that we would have three tunnels; in the event of a breakdown, people could move from one tunnel to the service tunnel and then, if need be, to the other main tunnel.

I said that it was an inherent part of our scheme that we did not need to attract such a high proportion of the cross-Channel traffic as to put out of business the existing ferry systems. We did not, in fact, intend to have all the cross-Channel eggs in one basket. But I did want to explain that our scheme would provide for a cheaper Channel crossing. At present the cost of crossing the Channel was very high and amounted to a surcharge for British commerce with the Continent. On average a goods vehicle had to pay £260 for the crossing. It cost nothing for such a vehicle to move between, say, France and Germany. I also explained to Mrs Thatcher the advantage the tunnel would have for trade to and from all parts of the British Isles and the Continent. It should be possible for freight to be moved much more easily and cheaply from the north of England, for example, to the south of the Continent by means of rail through the tunnel than by means of the present complication of a cross-Channel ferry. The tunnel would remove a serious handicap to our trade with the Community. I also spoke about the quick passenger service that the tunnel would provide between, say, the centre of London and the centre of Paris.

I told the Prime Minister that I understood that there was some concern that the tunnel might favour the south-east of England at the expense of the north or other parts of the British Isles. In fact this would not be so. As I had explained, because of the long and therefore economic rail hauls the tunnel should help all parts of the British Isles that trade with the Continent. Moreover, as regards construction, we would be providing work amounting to something of the order of £600 million for construction work spread all over the country.

Mrs Thatcher reiterated that she certainly had not been favouring any particular scheme. She was glad I had told her what ours consisted of. The main thing, she stressed, was that there should be a fixed link. Nothing exciting of this kind had been carried out by the British since the end of the Second World War. It was high time we became involved in an industrial enterprise of this scale. It also had highly important implications for our relations with Europe. She was therefore enthusiastic and would miss no chance of saying so.

On my way out of No. 10 I ran into the Foreign Secretary, Sir Geoffrey Howe. He told me that he did not favour any fixed link, as I knew. But he was being very good about it and was not raising objections if other people wanted to go ahead. I asked him if he would like me to come and explain our scheme, at which he shuddered. He said he did not want to hear about any of it. The best thing he could do was to lie low.

At the end of April 1985, I went again to France to see senior French officials in the President's office and in Crédit Lyonnais, and to call on the Minister of Town Planning, Housing and Transport, Paul Quilès. At the Elysée I saw Alain Boublil and Elisabeth Guigou. It was evident that they did not have detailed information about the essential features of the CTG scheme. They were also convinced that the Prime Minister favoured Euroroute. I think I helped to clarify their ideas and Boublil undertook to make a submission to the President himself on the subject. I was impressed by the unarrogant self-assurance of Madame Guigou. Beforehand everyone had told me how attractive she was. While not surprised to have this confirmed I had not expected to find someone so precise and so economical in expression. It was evident to me from my meetings at the President's office that they had doubts about the attitude of Francis Bouygues, one of the leading French contractors. A forceful personality, his influence seemed to extend from the realms of industry to those of banking and government. His hesitation seemed to be preventing the amalgamation of a constructors' and banking group with which we could associate.

At Crédit Lyonnais I ran into a good deal of pessimism about the chances of creating a consortium between the banks and the main constructors. When I saw Quilès I found him in a much more optimistic frame of mind. He gave me an assurance that the problem for us of finding a French partner would be resolved.

As so much seemed to turn on the attitude of Bouygues I decided to go to France again shortly afterwards to talk to him personally. This I did on 7 May. What emerged from my conversation with him (he was accompanied by Jean-Paul Parayre of Dumez, a French construction company that later joined CTG's French partners, and by executives from his own organization) was unexpected, except for the revelation of his own self-assurance. I had been led to believe various conflicting things about Bouygues' intentions: that he was committed to the tunnel and would be joining in a French consortium with us soon (Quilès); or that he wished to sit on the fence and not join either CTG or Euroroute so that he could get a slice of the action whichever was chosen (the Elysée and Crédit Lyonnais).

After I had explained the need for urgency and our requirement for a French partner as soon as possible, Bouygues said that he thought he might be able to join in preliminary talks in June but he would want to wait a couple of months before reaching a decision about which scheme to back. I asked him what there was in Euroroute that might attract him. He said that he did not favour Euroroute, which he had already examined, but he would like to give more attention to the pros and cons of a bridge. I said that, aside from cost, there was no question of a bridge being chosen by the British Government. In any case it could not be chosen without reference to the IMO and that would take time and probably lead to a negative answer.

Bouygues asked me what the hurry was. Why could we not all wait for a few years before coming to a decision? I replied that he had touched the point I particularly wanted to put to him; and I proceeded to deploy the argument about the political window of 1986, the Prime Minister's commitment and so on, that I need not record here. I said that in my view if we did not catch the present tide we would not see a fixed link this century. If that happened I would feel myself to blame; and I would consider him, Bouygues, likewise to blame, as would others.

Bouygues pressed me insistently on whether I personally was convinced that we could finance the tunnel. I said that I thought we could find the money for our present scheme but I had doubts about financing a drive-through tunnel. Bouygues agreed, adding that he did not think it feasible to expect people to drive over thirty kilometres in a tunnel. We then went on to discuss the tunnel in some detail; and the problems of organization and financing.

I said that I must press now for a commitment at a very early date. There could be no question of waiting until June. We had a vast task to be completed by 31 October. July and August were holidays in France. We could not proceed without the French. The French and British Governments would not choose Euroroute even if it was the only scheme submitted by the end of October. I wanted Bouygues therefore to ensure that we had a French partner within a week or two with whom we could get down to work. But he must renounce the idea of a bridge, which there was no possibility of the British Government accepting, as I knew from my meetings with British Ministers. If he sat on the fence there would be no fixed link of any kind. I added that I would be seeing the Prime Minister on 13 May and I would be ashamed if I had to confess that we were still nowhere with the French, particularly given that Mitterrand himself was so keen.

Bouygues said that what I had told him made it necessary for him to rethink his position. He understood what I had said about the timetable. He would be in touch with me by telephone or telex as soon as possible. On the way out he showed me the model of his offices to be built near Versailles. He promised me that on my next visit he would send his private plane, a British one, to pick me up at Roissy airport so that I would not have the long car journey. He was true to his word, for which I and the other members of the British team were frequently grateful in the months ahead.

During the next week or two Bouygues got together with the other French contractors favouring a tunnel and with the British constructors. I also heard that the French banks were in step with each other. But there was still no single body on the French side representing the necessary interests with whom we could sign up. This was delaying us. We were being severely criticized on all sides in Britain for losing the public relations battle while Sir Nigel Broackes seemed to be promoting his scheme with great aplomb. We appointed a public relations firm, Good Relations, and they produced all sorts of ideas for putting our project across; but the urgent need was to issue a brochure setting out the basic points of our project for widespread distribution and to hold a press conference. For both of these a French partner was essential. I therefore decided to go to Paris to see the chairman of Crédit Lyonnais, Jean Deflassieux.

At my meeting with Deflassieux on 20 May, I explained our urgent need to sign up with a French partner, and conveyed an official invitation to the French party to come to London, say on 19 June, to sign an agreement with us. The problem was complicated by internecine strife on the French side between the nationalized and private contractor groups; each wanted to join us, but without the other. I therefore asked the chairman of Crédit Lyonnais to do everything he could to bring the French interests together so that we could reach an umbrella agreement under which the specialists of the two countries could continue the task on which they were already embarked of working out a joint scheme. Deflassieux asked me what exactly I wanted him to do. I said that given Crédit Lyonnais' position, I wanted him to knock together the heads of the warring factions so that we could sign up with a French partner. He invited me to put this request to him in writing. I undertook to do this. He promised to get to work on the French side. But he seemed doubtful whether we would be able to meet the deadline of 19 June. He thought it might be better to talk in terms of the second half of June. He also thought that it would be much easier for the French if we were able to go to Paris to sign. I said that we could do this. Deflassieux suggested that any project which was sponsored by something called Trafalgar House would not be likely to find favour in France. At this stage we did not know, nor, fortunately, did the French, that Waterloo would be British Rail's terminal for the new train link.

When, a fortnight or so later, there was still no further sign of progress from France I wrote to Deflassieux and also to Quilès and to Boublil in the President's office. Still no response. Indeed the next sign of life I received from a potential French partner was an urgent request to visit him from Jean-Paul Parayre, who had been alongside Bouygues when I had visited him on 7 May[5] and who now looked likely to become the chairman of whatever group was formed on the French side. I was told that there was a crisis within the French team jeopardizing the chances of our signing up with a French partner in the foreseeable future. So I made arrangements with Q. Morris to go with him to Paris on 17 June, both to see Parayre and to touch base with Crédit Lyonnais, who wanted to have discussions on the financial outlook.

Marcel Sarmet, whom we were to see frequently over the next few months, was our host at a lunch given for us by Crédit Lyonnais at the Drouant, a restaurant that has something of the atmosphere of a London club, except in its incomparable food. They were pessimistic, as were the Banque Nationale de Paris, whom we were also to have in our joint consortium. Our French hosts did not appear to think there was much I could do to solve the problem; nevertheless they hoped I would try. When Q. Morris and I went on after lunch to see Parayre it was not really a question of devising a solution. He

[5] See p. 26.

proved to be much more forthcoming than we had been led to expect. True, there were serious difficulties on the French side but Parayre in his charming and practical way gave no impression of being overcome by them. I deliberately avoided probing him about the French uncertainties and decided to act on the assumption that things would come all right. I handed him the text of a draft agreement that I hoped that we could both sign very soon. I said that I was open to any suggestions he might have for amending the wording, which was very loosely drafted. I explained our plan to launch our scheme publicly on 2 July. I hoped he might be able to come to London and sign at the time of the launch. This would provide a peg for the media. It would make it difficult to get our scheme off to a promising start if we were unable to say that we had a French partner. Parayre and his colleagues glanced at the text and showed no inclination either to question the principle or to criticize the detail.

We went on to discuss other things including the problem of raising money, upon which Q. Morris gave some erudite information. We also talked about the nature of our scheme. Parayre spoke, as the Crédit Lyonnais had predicted he would, about the doubts that still existed on the French side about whether to have two seven-metre tunnels or one tunnel of eleven metres. SNCF were apparently favouring the latter. I said that we had done a lot of research and were in no doubt about the superiority of two tunnels. We also stressed the urgent need for a conclusion. I derived the impression that Parayre agreed with us but had to take the line that the question must remain open because of the views of the other people on the French side. Referring to the continuing friction between the contractors on the one hand and the banks on the other, Parayre suggested that we might have to sign up with a French partner which excluded the banks. I asked him to be sure not to form such a consortium.

At this stage in our meeting, and indeed throughout it, we went in for a good deal of light-hearted banter. I think this helped. We had established a sound basis and by the end of our talk I got the clear impression that Parayre would be ready to sign up with us on behalf of a comprehensive French group within the time scale. Even at this early stage I was struck by the calibre of the people we were talking to on the French side – Parayre himself, Jean Renault (of Spie Batignolles), Philippe Montagner (of Bouygues) and Marcel Sarmet and Jean-Jacques Hessig (both of Crédit Lyonnais) – a sentiment that grew steadily as we worked closely with them over the next months. All of us, not least the female members, on the British side were captivated from the outset by the charm and courtesy of the French legal adviser, Hervé Charrin. At any rate, I came away from the first meeting feeling greatly encouraged: no doubt grave problems lay ahead but on the personal level I relished the prospect of dealing with Parayre and his clever and far from solemn team.

I have no idea how our French partners found us. From time to time they would make an agreeable remark about how phlegmatic we were in the face of crisis, but I think that what they really meant by this was that they saw us as unaware – rather as Soult found Wellington at Salamanca, complaining to Napoleon afterwards that he 'had the English beat but they had been such fools, they had not realized it and refused to run'. When, as often happened, we made some gaffe, the French would brush it aside with a remark about English humour.

The Launch

Everything came together so well and so quickly that we were able to plan for the French party to come to London on 1 July, to sign an agreement with us that evening at Suffolk Street, to dine with us at the Garrick and then to join us for the press launch the following day. But as so often happens in this story, the arrangements went awry and the day of the French arrival seethed with drama, both comical and tragic, sometimes a mixture of both. The French had asked us to make bookings in a hotel and to lay on transport. This proved difficult as the hotels were full. It was the time of Wimbledon. With great difficulty my secretary Mary Cozens managed to book Parayre into Brown's Hotel and the rest of the party elsewhere. This shook some of the latter who said that they could not be housed separately from their chairman. We explained that there was no more room in Brown's. We suggested that they might do better by asking the French Ambassador to do the bookings. That settled it, and they accepted what we had arranged. But what we had arranged turned into a mirage because the hotel had overbooked and when the French party arrived they found they had no rooms. Mary Cozens hurried round to placate them and to try to find accommodation elsewhere. When she reached the party she was told what they thought of British hotels, British efficiency and the Entente Cordiale generally. Accommodation was eventually found, but meanwhile the cars had been lost.

I have always thought that among the most difficult things in diplomacy are transport and the delivery of messages. I soon became involved in both. I was changing at home prior to going to the signing ceremony and then on to dinner when the telephone rang. Parayre, who had travelled separately, was on the line from Heathrow in a state of some indignation because the car that I had promised to send to pick him up was not there. 'Are you sure?' I asked, and added feebly that the car 'should have been there', hoping that I had got the conditional correct in French, for this tense is as crucial as it is difficult in a crisis. We agreed that in the circumstances the only sensible course for Parayre was to take a taxi from the airport to the hotel. I would then arrange for my car and driver to bring him from there to Suffolk Street for the signing. I apologized profusely for the *dégringolade*. Having finished this uncomfortable telephone conversation, I continued to dress for the evening event and decided to write, and leave at Brown's Hotel, a note of apology and welcome for Parayre. Some twenty minutes later I delivered this message to the hotel and was told that Parayre had just arrived. I managed to see him as he was signing in for his room and did my best to assure him of our ability to muddle through.

However, none of this had presented as much difficulty as was posed by a last-minute problem concerning the text that we were to sign. The French were insisting that the agreement should state specifically that the two parties had agreed to collaborate on an 'exclusive basis' for the purpose of submitting a proposal to the two Governments. The lawyers employed by some of the British contractors argued that such 'exclusivity' would be contrary to European Community law. They could not therefore agree to my signing an agreement on the terms insisted upon by the French. Throughout 1 July, the day set aside for signature, I was bombarded by telexes forbidding me to sign on the basis that was alone acceptable to the French. An idea was advanced that we should sign two agreements, one public, omitting the word 'exclusive', the other private with the word included. Another suggestion was that the agreement be accompanied by an exchange of letters which would say the opposite. None of these brainwaves could possibly have been acquiesced in by both the French and British sides. I had checked earlier with the Foreign and Commonwealth Office, whose advisers confirmed that our agreement, which related to collaborating to submit a plan, rather than to carrying it out, was unlikely to lay us open to a legal charge under Article 85 of the Treaty of Rome, which was what the British contractors' lawyers feared. But as I probed more deeply into what lay behind the contractors' objections, I gained the impression that they may have been seeking to leave their options open should things not work out as planned.

I managed to get hold of John Reeve, who represented the contractors on our executive committee. He was robust and said that I should go ahead and sign and he would take responsibility for any adverse consequences. So I ignored the negative telexes and devoted the last few minutes to making the Board room at Suffolk Street ready for signature – and to ensuring that the transport arrangements for the French team were as foolproof as possible.

Eventually we all joined up at Suffolk Street for the signing. This was accompanied by generous speeches and ample glasses of Pol Roger champagne. We were photographed in front of portraits of HM the Queen and President Mitterrand, this backcloth having required last-minute improvisation because the Board room had been used hitherto by a Dutch–British organization and we had to substitute President Mitterrand's photograph for that of the Queen of the Netherlands, the sort of legerdermain for which our team invariably showed remarkable flair.

The text of the agreement was short and simple. After listing the participants to the proposal for a Channel fixed link it stated that 'France Manche represented by Monsieur Jean-Paul Parayre, and CTG, represented by Sir Nicholas Henderson, agree to collaborate on an exclusive basis for the purpose of preparing and submitting such a proposal and to secure concessions from the said French and British Governments. . . .' At the same time we agreed to establish an Anglo-French Executive Committee to meet every fortnight, alternately in Britain and France. This was to become an important engine for moving our project forward. We also created a number of joint specialist committees – technical, financial, economic, legal, and so on. Shortly afterwards a Joint Venture Agreement was signed between the constructors' organizations on either side.

In dwelling on the difficulties with the French I must avoid giving the impression that all was harmonious among the British players. Our Board meetings at this stage were untidy and unconstructive, serving more as a platform for rows, so it seemed to me, than as a forum for solutions. There were running battles between contractors and banks and between the directors and the management. The need for a single driving mechanism, smaller than the Board and capable of deciding and acting quickly, was glaring. We therefore established an executive committee. I decided that I would have to take the chair of this if we were to get the work done in time. However, I ran into opposition from some members of the Board who thought that the chairman of the Board and the chairman of the executive committee should be different people. I said that I could not provide the impulse that the project needed unless at this stage I also played an executive role. Later, when the project was further advanced and there was a full-time managing director representing both the British and the French owners, the chairman obviously would hand over to him the main executive responsibility. I cannot say that I put this matter to a vote. It was my practice to avoid votes of the directors at all times. But I assumed their acquiescence – and also grew an extra skin.

Under the leadership of Quentin Morris our financial team were by midsummer moving into higher gear. They had to produce a provisional information memorandum intended for use in canvassing potential lenders of money and purchasers of equity. The auguries for this were more favourable than they had appeared to be the previous year at the time of the publication of the report of the Anglo-French Financing Group. The cost and revenue figures now made the scheme look more viable. The response of the markets was more positive than the banks had expected, even though it was clear that there would be no government involvement. The prognosis for attracting equity capital had become brighter and a larger equity basis was a cornerstone of the financial plan. It would encourage the banks to undertake long-term lending. Furthermore, previous ideas about the limits of the market had been radically altered in late 1984 by the success of the British Telecom flotation; besides, the share market had become increasingly bullish. I came to be impressed, as also were the two governments, by the commitments we obtained from the banks for loans amounting to £4 billion, and their opinion that we would be justified in submitting proposals on the basis that we would be able to secure £1 billion from equity.

It is difficult to exaggerate the importance of our financing package in determining the outcome. I do not say that the British Government's financial advisers necessarily thought it brilliant, but it shone in comparison with that of the others. I always believed that Euroroute would have failed at the financial fence if, improbably, their scheme had proved acceptable to Ministers in other respects.

An important difference between French and British practice emerged in the realm of banking. I suspected that what mattered to the French banks was not so much the apparent financial viability of this scheme or the other, about which there could of course be much argument, as the attitude and decision of the French Government. This was not, I think, because the French banks are nationalized but because they believed that their Government, if they opted for a particular scheme, would ensure that it did not fail. The imprimatur of the French Government was tantamount to a political guarantee that funds would be made available. For the sake of argument, had the decision gone in favour of Euroroute, French banks would have been found who were ready to put up the money, however financially shaky the scheme, because they would deduce that the Government in the end would stick behind it.

As was to happen so frequently in the history of our project, suddenly clouds were to appear out of a blue sky and to threaten the whole outlook. Michael Gordon and I were to become, if not accustomed to, at least philosophical about, the successive storms that shook us – one week public relations, the next organization, then our French partners, and now, at this time, on the eve of the launch of the whole project, a tempest rather than a storm that blew up over prospective traffic for the tunnel. Our financial advisers appeared suddenly to get cold feet and to be unprepared to express confidence that the tunnel could be financed from private sources. I pointed out that it was a bit late in the day to be having these doubts, and that nothing had changed since the banks had said that they were sure that they could find the money without resort to governments. The advisers replied that what had changed was the forecast of traffic, and hence of revenue, which made it much more difficult to be sure of raising money from the market, particularly equity. I rejoined that any estimate of traffic, whether freight or passengers, for the mid-1990s was bound to be hazardous. It was very hard to judge what the total traffic would be at that time and how much would be diverted to a tunnel if one existed. New means of transport, for example jumbo jets, were apt to generate traffic that would not have been there had they not existed. In the brochure and the video film which were to be launched on 2 July, statements of confidence about the financing were made. The banks had been aware of this for weeks so it was annoying, to put it mildly, if they were now to say at the last minute that they could not go along with such wording. I pointed out that the French had confidence in our traffic figures, which indeed had been put together after a great deal of research by our consultants, Wilbur Smith.

From the talk I had had with Alistair Dick of Wilbur Smith, I had learned that the Government were not expecting precise traffic forecasts before deciding whether a scheme was likely to be financeable; their criterion was going to be whether the figures were 'not unreasonable', a double negative which was not just the reflection of official caution but was intended to allow a certain degree of flexibility. We were never told what figures the Government thought 'not unreasonable' because it was government policy not to publish their traffic appraisals. This caginess was never explained but I surmised that they feared their figures might prove to be wildly wrong, as nearly all government forecasts of traffic have been from time immemorial. I suggested to our financial advisers that they had better feign illness and stay away from the press launch rather than turn up and pour cold water on what was after all an essential plank in our scheme, one which had been put into position after considerable thought. The view of the rest of us was that the traffic estimates could not be regarded as so categorically negative as to oblige us to conclude at this juncture that we could not finance the scheme. We were therefore going ahead and submitting our bid. We might as well, therefore, comport ourselves with confidence rather than pessimism; indeed the only attitude that would generate the money would be one of confidence.

The traffic storm blew itself out as suddenly as it had arisen. We heard no more about it. Our financial advisers came along to the press launch and were as resolute as the rest of us. Indeed Q. Morris described our task of raising money as a mere 'doddle' compared with the financing of a major North Sea oil project. I opened the press conference by saying that opera singers used to be renowned for the number of their farewell performances. The Channel tunnel by contrast had acquired a reputation for frequent overtures upon which the curtain never rose: 'Why then is it different now? Why am I confident in inviting you here today that we are at last going to see light at the beginning and end of the tunnel? Firstly, because the leaders of the British and French Governments want a fixed link – they are indeed enthusiastic about it and want it now. The political will is there.' The second note I struck was that ours was the best scheme for vehicles as for trains. What we were proposing to construct would be a rolling motorway for the twenty-first century with departures every five minutes in a modern shuttle service. It would be an advanced but practical method of transport for the high-technology age. Existing means of crossing the Channel could not meet the growing demand. Our scheme could be financed and built privately by an Anglo-French consortium without resort to public money. Jean-Paul Parayre sat beside me at the press conference and expressed unqualified confidence in our joint project. We were launched.

There was prominent television and press coverage, national and regional. *The Times* published a leader about the prospects for private enterprise, without coming down clearly in favour of any particular scheme. Under the heading 'The Curtain Starts to Rise' the *Financial Times* carried an article saying that this was the week people had been waiting for since Napoleon Bonaparte first promoted the idea of a link. They presented it as a struggle between the Channel tunnel and the Euroroute schemes; and this was how the public were led to see it for the next four months, as a bilateral battle between the two projects with Broackes and me in the roles of Tweedledum and Tweedledee.

Submission

We were, of course, trying to do too much in too short a space of time. During the next four months, up to 31 October, I was agitated by the prospect of having to complete so vast a task by that date even as I was assuaged by the thought that the pressure would not go on beyond that time – an assumption that turned out to be completely false.

Despite recurring doubts in the minds of some of the contractors' leaders about the financial validity of the scheme in the absence of a governmental guarantee (Broackes, however, was promising to raise twice our sum), and the continuing inadequacy of our organization, we made progress at the working level. We had useful meetings with the French about the width and nature of the shuttle and what sort of toilets it should have. To a proposal which was put to me that because Channel transit was so short there would be no need for toilets I was able to insert my little contribution to the facilities of the project by saying: 'There must be toilets.'

As I have said, relations between the directors and the management creaked. As the representatives of the owners who were putting up the money and bearing the risks, the directors felt that they did not have adequate control, particularly over expenditure. Every meeting of the Board produced a wrangle on the budget. The main trouble, I think, was that the management were taking on too many highly paid consultants without prior authority from the owners. 'We may be prepared to risk £25–30 million to get this project off the ground' was how the point was put to me, 'but only if we can exercise control as well as see reasonable expectation of profit.'

The contractors were adamant against bringing in at this stage any additional owners, for example Vickers, Ferranti or Hawker Siddeley, who might seek to take a slice of the action, thereby reducing the profits of the original owners. But they acknowledged that they were not providers of equity themselves, so by implication they accepted that there would have to be new owners eventually if we were to raise the £2.1 billion the scheme was going to cost. But they wanted us to find providers of pure equity, rather than people who would be putting up money partly because they would be hoping to get some of the work. They also pointed out that under European Community rules 30 per cent of all deals in the Community had to be open to subcontractors.

There was one important respect in which the directors came to share the views of the management. Hitherto thay had favoured bringing in an operator, such as P&O, to run the shuttle. But they concluded that this would be a mistake since the consortium would be sacrificing a source of revenue once the tunnel was built. Better for the consortium to operate the shuttle themselves, bringing in consultants as necessary. P&O, incidentally, were not prepared to join us; I saw Sir Jeffery Sterling twice, but he did not wish to commit himself.

The internal strife came to a head in September when I was out of the country for a short holiday. On my return I was told that an Extraordinary Meeting of the Board had been held in my absence. The directors had complained about the inadequacies of the management and the delays in producing drafts for the submission to Governments. Certain changes in high-level staff had therefore been decided upon, the Board's intention being to deprive all 'outsiders' of any executive power. Aware that the directors had for long been receiving biased accounts of what was going on in the organization, I was not best pleased that they should have come to these conclusions in my absence. I quite accepted that there were shortcomings in the management. But these largely arose from the reluctance of the owners to delegate or appoint sufficient highly qualified people with the necessary dedication to help at the tunnel face in Hammersmith; moreover, the management were held up by the lack of decisions by the owners. If money was being spent without adequate control, the answer would have been to appoint a suitable accountant.

If this narrative is to be complete, albeit as a personal account, I cannot conceal that I contemplated the idea of resigning the chairmanship. However sententious it sounds now, I have to confess that I nevertheless had in the forefront of my mind the importance of the project itself. Personal feelings therefore had to be kept in their place. It was no good being too touchy, and, besides, I realized that I had to take some of the blame myself. Surely I had failed to exert sufficient authority over the Board. I thought it advisable to have it out with one or two of the directors. I was determined to save Melville Guest, whom the old Turks in the organization had evidently hoped to demote, presumably because he was a newcomer. I was uncompromising with Frank Gibb and he was understanding with me. Guest was reinstated. Our row cleared the air. From then on at Board meetings I began to sense an improvement in the way we operated. The size of the meetings was limited and as time went on acrimony died down; certainly my experience of handling such things also grew, and as I look back now, those gatherings at Suffolk Street begin to take on a rosy hue. The top executives of the parent companies increasingly attended in person despite the great demands this made on their time. Our Board room could only seat about twenty people, which was a great advantage. Our needs in the form of coffee, and occasionally something stronger, were beautifully attended to by Fiona Morris, the abigail, the impresario, the indispensable secretary-in-chief of our headquarters in Suffolk Street. The proceedings benefited from the frank way everybody spoke about each other. At one point I quoted to the directors from T. S. Eliot's *The Cocktail Party:* 'You will find that you survive humiliation. And that's an experience of incalculable value.' I said that I was grateful for the experience.

This experience had also taught me to regularize my own financial position. Hitherto I had requested and received no pay. It dawned on me that nevertheless I was earning something – the contempt of the directors. I came to realize that if, in their eyes, I did not judge myself as worth anything, I could not expect them to attach much value to me; and that in the business world, unlike Government service, if you don't ask you don't get. So, I asked. From then on I received a salary, one that was fair but not excessive, given the commitment of my time.

It would not be obvious to anyone outside our organization how we spent such long hours at the frequent Board meetings, both at this stage and right up to the mandate. We did not, for instance, talk about many of the subjects in which people outside showed most interest – security, rabies, loading, traction, employment opportunities and how the environment would be affected – but what we talked about a great deal were the terms of the contract between the owners and the contractors (probably the most intractable problem of all), or the raising of different tranches of equity, or our own management structure, or, of course, the budget. One feature of our proceedings that distinguished them at all times from any governmental activity I had ever been associated with was, of course, the profit motive. Everything we did had to be geared to that objective. It was no good working out the design of a beautiful tunnel or devising an alluring shuttle unless we could raise the money from the market and to do this the project had to promise a good financial return when it was in operation. Hence the enormous amount of time we devoted to the scale of tariffs and the agreement with the British and French railways.

This was the season of presentations. Together with Michael Gordon, Tony Gueterbock and Don Hunt, I spent a lot of time in mid-summer in the basement of a hotel not far from the Houses of Parliament offering hospitality to members of Parliament – described as 'finger food' and meagre beyond the call of incorruptibility – showing them our ten-minute film and answering questions. Many members of both Houses received our illustrated brochure with an offer of a cassette to help them while away the long summer hours.

At a meeting with Michael Heseltine, the Secretary of State for Defence, I was reassured that the tunnel would present no problems for the country's security. A talk with John Smith, MP, Opposition Spokesman on Trade and Industry, gave me an insight into his great ability and into Labour Party attitudes more generally. Later meetings with David Steel and David Owen left me heartened about the likely reaction of the Alliance to a fixed link. From the many meetings I had with various committees of the House of Commons and House of Lords I was struck by the fact that, although there were serious objections from some members who feared that their constituency or regional interests might be threatened and although I realized that there was by no means a consensus in favour of any particular scheme, there was no doubt about the curiosity the idea had evoked. 'Is it really going to come off this time?' seemed to be a frequently expressed or implied question.

We also gave a special presentation there to senior officials of the Civil Service. I took the opportunity of turning their questions by asking them what length and type of submission would be most convenient for Whitehall. The answer I got was, predictably, that it should be as short as possible with detail packed into appendices. Andrew Lyall, Under-Secretary at the Department of Transport, spoke for Whitehall. He was probably the most important senior official with whom we dealt, both in the period leading up to the submission and then in the tense months before the award of the mandate. He never showed any favour towards us, but his very frankness was invaluable. We always knew where we were with him even when our prospects looked bleak; he answered our queries without equivocation and he certainly never gave us any encouragement. What mattered – little though it is my business to say so – was his unremitting application to the multifarious tasks, for which, since he was a high-minded official, I am sure that he did not expect any gratitude. I take the opportunity here of saluting his undemonstrative but indispensable contribution. I must also mention Dr Chris Woodman, omniscient, smiling and inscrutable, an intellectually outstanding member of the assessment team, the Jack Nicholson of the Department of Transport, though fortunately with more hair and unfortunately with a less lecherous look; and, later, John Noulton who picked up the threads and displayed a remarkably equable temperament. Our lives were inexorably entwined with theirs for many months and I should not like their praises to go unsung merely because they were working as officials, whereas the project was a private one.

I gave lunch one day to the editor of a prominent newspaper who happened to live near the South Coast and therefore claimed considerable expertise on the working, or non-working, of the southern line of British Rail. 'If you should want to know', he said to me, 'how our friends from the Caribbean run the rail when there's a *déménagement* late in the evening, just join me at Waterloo to catch the 10.40 to Ashford. Then you'll see what you're up against trying to incorporate this line into a rapid rail system such as will be required by the tunnel.'

Our plans did not assume that there would be a new rail-link between the coast and London of the kind which had caused such consternation during the previous link negotiations in the 1970s. However, the people of Kent had no doubt that our scheme was going to have major environmental, economic and employment consequences for their area. There was no doubt in our minds either that we would have to pay a great deal of attention to this, a requirement put upon us in any case by the guidelines. Tony Gueterbock was given responsibility for co-ordinating presentations and engaging the necessary consultants – to advise on everything conceivable, including hydrology, archaeology, ecology and spoil. Our studies, and discussions conducted by Gueterbock with debonair enthusiasm, took account of the changing pattern of transport that the tunnel would create, the likely economic development arising from the terminal at Cheriton in Kent and the visible impacts of such a terminal and of other works. Careful examination was made of the impact of our scheme on the ports and labour markets during and following completion of the tunnel. I sent an account of what we were doing under a personal letter to Kenneth Baker, Secretary of State for the Environment, informing him that we had commissioned eighteen specialist reports on the environment, all of which were being made available to public libraries and interested institutions in Kent.

We fully shared the Government's fear that a public enquiry would delay legislation and therefore put the link in jeopardy, and believed that the proposed parliamentary Hybrid Bill and our own very thorough consultations would give members of the public ample opportunity to express their views. Those who persisted in calling for a public enquiry tended to be opponents of any fixed link. Apart from the delay, amounting to years, that a public enquiry would create, the Government objected to it on the grounds that such a procedure would be inappropriate. What they meant, as I found myself explaining to many enquirers and protesters, was that this was a subject of national, rather than local, significance, and the place for decision on such matters was the highest court of the realm, that is to say the British Parliament. A dialogue was established with the local authorities and with many statutory bodies. Gueterbock organized debates with a wide range of local audiences. In October 1985 the CTG produced a brochure of over 100 pages on our consultations in Kent; that should give an idea of the amount of care we devoted to this aspect of our scheme.

Less successful, yet more memorable, was a conference laid on in London for representatives of the foreign press. With considerable fanfare it was announced that we would be showing our film, following this up with questions and discussion. There was a wonderful turn-out, and looking from the platform of the hall I was reminded of a meeting of the United Nations. But as I was about to start the proceedings I was informed that the film had been forgotten. I was assured that it was on its way from Hammersmith. However, our time was up before it arrived, and Sir Nigel Broackes took over the conference with his film, which though less persuasive was at least available.

Apart from Broackes and Euroroute we had a competitor, prominent in all press and television presentations, in Lord Layton and his scheme for a cross-Channel bridge. This was an eye-catching idea and I could not help wishing to myself that such a beautiful concept were practical; but I had derived the clear impression that the meteorological, maritime and technical snags were regarded by the authorities as insuperable.

To advertise, or not to advertise, that was the question much discussed then and for the next six months or so. Throughout that time we were criticized for failing to get ourselves across to the country as a whole, and there is no doubt, judged by the questions fired at us from all sides and from the adverse line taken about us by many of the leading newspapers, that few of the people who took an interest in the subject seemed to have much knowledge of the details of our scheme. This may not have mattered all that much, I philosophized, because what was essential was not to wage a permanent offensive on all fronts but to focus on persuading the twenty-one members of the Cabinet, when they came to take a decision some time around the turn of the year, that they should award the mandate to us. It was no good peaking too early and I had an idea that this was what Euroroute had done. Obviously public and parliamentary opinion would affect the Cabinet's decision; but to impinge on the minds of Ministers, and to do so at the right moment, that was our objective. We did not consider that advertising would help us to achieve it. Flexilink, representing the ferry industry, the Dover Harbour Board and all those who were against any fixed link, launched a bluff advertising campaign with such slogans as 'The Channel Tunnel: the black hole that will put Britain in the red', or 'Hired by the Channel Tunnel: 3,500 employees. Fired by the Channel Tunnel: 40,000 employees'. I am not sure that such slogans did us much harm, though they were grist to the mill of those who accused us of being laggards in public relations. Fortunately we came to an understanding with Sir Nigel Broackes to avoid engaging in an advertising war. This saved both our organizations a lot of money.

At the end of September 1985 I went to Paris to attend our French partners' press launch at the Automobile Club in the Place de la Concorde. It was well organized, thanks a great deal, I am sure, to the efforts of Corinne Bouygues, the daughter of Francis Bouygues. She was in charge of France Manche's public relations. An arresting, fair-haired figure, she was a chip off the old block in energy and self-confidence, and as she swung from one palatial room to another of the Automobile Club she struck me as very much *dans son assiette* and I was glad it was also ours.

At the press conference I was called upon to *'faire quelques remarques'*. As so often I could not resist trying to make a joke or two and as always they fell fairly flat. For some time Paris had been intrigued by a strange work of art: the beautiful Pont Neuf had been wrapped up by some artist in material that looked like hessian. Whether they liked it or not the Parisians were certainly interested in this gimmick. When, therefore, I came to speak about the merits of the various projects for a fixed link I said that I had to admit that compared with a bridge our tunnel might have the disadvantage that it could not be wrapped up. Despite the lack of response to this *jeu d'esprit* I decided to risk another. The French Government had been in trouble for some time over the sinking in New Zealand of the ship, the *Rainbow Warrior*, for which they admitted responsibility. In doing this the Prime Minister had said that the truth was cruel, '*la verité est cruelle*'. I therefore concluded my remarks by saying that ours was the best scheme, that it was the only one technically viable and financially feasible and that, as I am sure my audience would agree, '*la verité est tunnel*'. Again, not exactly a riotous response.

Afterwards a British journalist who had worked in France for years said that he was only surprised that I should have expected the penny to drop. 'Do you not understand after all your time in France, old man, that they don't have the same humour as we have?'

Shortly after the conference I called on Alain Boublil in the President's office. I began by referring to the impressive presentation that had taken place in the Automobile Club; and I also mentioned the short time available to us before the joint submission had to be made to the two Governments. We were therefore working extremely hard and I wanted to be sure that I had a full picture of everything that was going on. I would therefore like to learn anything he had to tell me about the attitude of the President to a fixed link.

Boublil said that the answer was quite simple. The President was enthusiastic about the idea and wanted a decision taken as soon as possible so that progress could be made. The only hesitation on the French side concerned the British. There continued to be some doubts whether the British would ever take the step involved in committing themselves to a fixed link. But there was no doubt whatever of the President's strong wish to have one. I replied that the President should be in no doubt about the Prime Minister's enthusiasm. I had spoken to many members of the British Cabinet on the subject and they were all supportive. There was no question that there would be a large parliamentary majority in favour of the link. I did not therefore think that the President need nourish any doubts about British interest in the project. Boublil explained that the French, because they were so eager for a decision in favour of a link, would listen very carefully to whatever the British had to say.

In the many meetings we had with our French partners we were trying on both sides to accommodate very different business and political practices, apart altogether from the problems of language. *'Qu'est ce que c'est ce, Joint et Several Liability?'* Jean-Paul Parayre asked me with a shrug, as if to denote the absurdity of the concept. Later, when we tried to explain the complications and delays in our parliamentary procedure he expressed astonishment at our 'Hybrid Bill', pronounced, of course, without the aspirate, and as if he were referring derisorily to the hero of a Wild West film.

Shortly before we made our submission to the two Governments I attended a promotion lunch in Paris which was outstanding for the blunt speaking of Francis Bouygues. Denouncing Euroroute for being not a link but a series of obstacles he declared, *'L'Euroroute c'est une absurdité.'* This rallied our troops. I was under constant pressure from our own people to 'take the gloves off', or 'to stop pussy-footing the enemy'. All the same I thought it better to avoid vituperation, while quite happy that Bouygues should have a fling.

On 30 October, the eve of our deadline for the submission, Jean-Paul Parayre flew over by private plane to Stansted airfield to sign various documents to be conveyed to the Governments the following day. Despite the extreme reluctance of the authorities, I managed with the rest of our group to go out on to the tarmac to greet Parayre's plane. He told me with a grave expression that there were many outstanding problems that would have to be solved before signature. Could we therefore go somewhere to discuss them? We walked towards the hangar piled high with crates and equipment and busy with men whizzing about on fork-lift trucks. Leading off from this was a room with broken-down chairs and a coffee machine and one or two airport employees sitting about disconsolately. I asked Parayre whether this would do for our meeting, but he said no, it would take some time and anyhow we could not do it in front of these people. I wandered out into the hangar. All exits were blocked by barbed wire. We would have to go out through customs and make our way to the lounge of the main airport. The VIP lounge of Stansted was seven miles away and might well no longer be open. So in a fleet of cars we rushed through the lanes to the main airport entrance. I led the way to the restaurant, only to find there nothing but small tables with four fixed chairs around each. However, one of our party spotted a long table at the far end of the restaurant and this we commandeered for our negotiations.

The difficulties did not strike me as all that insurmountable. They related, as had so many of our problems over many weeks, to the terms and timing of the contract between the owners and the contractors. The French and British contractors wanted this tied up as tightly as possible before the submission. The owners' interests were watched over by independent consultants.

In order to ease our work in the unpromising setting of the self-service restaurant I went to the bar to order some wine. 'Not till six o'clock,' the barmaid told me with that look of pleasurable rejection that makes me wonder why Napoleon ever called us a nation of shopkeepers. So we started with tea. Then when six o'clock struck I returned to the bar. No, they had no bottles of wine, just half bottles. I looked at the restaurant menu which mentioned bottles of wine. Yes, I could order these; which I did. But when she brought two bottles and eight glasses to our table the barmaid informed me, with renewed pleasure, that she had no corkscrew. I think the French were as delighted by this evidence of our culinary incompetence as they were disappointed at not getting a drink. However, one of our drivers came to the rescue. The bottles were opened. I ordered two more and some sandwiches; and these refreshments together with frequent telephone calls to the banks in London and Paris enabled us to conclude our negotiations well before midnight.

The haze of Stansted Muscadet that drifts over the retina of memory does not, I must say, obscure the clear impression I retain from these hectic last-minute negotiations that, if the French and British really have some interest and aim in common, they will find a way of surmounting all those much-trumpeted cultural and traditional differences.

I will not try to describe the last-minute scramble by the British and French teams to assemble our proposal. One or two figures will give an idea of the scale of effort. Our project filled eleven volumes and contained 2,500 pages, every word equally valid in English and French. In the editing process of the last three weeks 10,000 amendments had to be incorporated in the text, which ran through fifteen versions. It was not many months since the French and British teams had favoured and worked on different tunnel concepts and configurations, so agreement by the end of October on a single theme portrayed technological as well as diplomatic tractability, for which the combined team of constructors deserved high credit. It also owed much to the readiness of the French to accept English as the working language. As a general rule neither the French nor the English pride themselves on their knowledge of foreign languages; but I have to confess that in the world of the tunnel the French far outstripped us in linguistic ability.

Lively in my memory is the time I spent drafting the summary. I undertook this myself, thinking that it was one way in which I could help and believing that the summary was all that most Ministers would be likely to read. In retrospect I realize I was naïve not to see that some people in our organization who had been working full-time there for a long period might well think that this was their task and that I should leave it to them. It was one of the lessons I was to learn about the difference between working for Government and working for private enterprise. In the official world drafting is seen as an anonymous, even a collective, task to which everyone contributes without personal attribution. But the impression I came to derive of the business world was that competition prevails both inside and outside the organization. If I had understood this better at the time I think I would have been less disturbed by the friction created by Melville Guest's appointment.[6] That he could make a unique contribution to the putting together of our document did not, in human terms, compensate for the feeling that he was usurping the functions of others. Perhaps also I should have been less surprised by the frankness of the comments on my own drafting of the summary. Some of these were far from flattering. One piece of advice I received was that I should start all over again and completely recast it. A member of the Board, who I am sure was not grinding any personal axe, told me that he thought it was very dull. I had to agree with him. In defence I pleaded that the subject did not lend itself to poetry. Nevertheless he had got under my skin, and I tried to liven up the document by inserting a preface which put the link in a wider perspective. This ran as follows:

> If the peoples of Western Europe are to forge together their separate economies and exploit their varying skills so as to achieve their maximum capabilities by the end of this century, they will have to create fast new means of communication between densely populated regions. Many of these regions are separated by natural barriers – the Alps, the Pyrenees or

[6] See p. 18.

the Channel. Great improvements have been made in traditional means of transport – motorways and high-speed trains – but new ideas are required to overcome the remaining geographical barriers and increasing transport demands of Western Europe. This is particularly true of the Channel, where traffic is expected to double between now and the end of the century.

At any rate the summary was beautifully illustrated and produced – a document that stood on its own, describing all the main features of our project in non-technical language. In moments when I allowed my fancy to take flight I would imagine copies of our shining summary being offered as quaint mementos to passengers comfortably seated in the panelled Pullman cars of the first train to pass through the tunnel in eight years' time.

Before the great day much discussion had taken place between our organization and the Department of Transport about the delivery of our project, which was so voluminous that it would have to arrive by special van; there was also much toing and froing about the private meeting and photo-opportunity to take place between proposers and the Secretary of State. When, as arranged, I arrived in the van at the entrance to the department in Marsham Street we were held up for some time before being told that we had come to the wrong place. With some difficulty we reversed and entered by another gate. I got out and walked to the door which had been indicated to me, but no, it was the wrong door. I should go to entrance No. 3. By now we had overrun the extremely precise timetable that had been arranged, so I hurried to No. 3 where the security guard looked blank when I said that I had an appointment with the Secretary of State. He turned to an attendant beside him who, looking equally baffled, picked up a dog-eared telephone directory which she began to flick through. 'Who do you say you are seeing?', she asked.

'The Secretary of State – the Minister – Mr Nicholas Ridley,' I replied, hoping that one of these gilded pennies would drop. But no, neither she nor the security guard had heard of any of them. 'You know I am late,' I said. 'Please tell me which is the main floor, I will make my way there myself.' They muttered something about the twelfth floor and I hurried towards the lifts, meeting on my way Sir Nigel Broackes who seemed to have entered the building and to be making in the right direction with customary aplomb.

The meeting in Ridley's room was attended by Sir Nigel Broackes, Lord Layton (chairman of the Bridge Scheme) and James Sherwood – with a last-minute project, Expressway, for a tunnel for both road and rail vehicles – and myself. Like exhibitors at a horticultural show who arrive proudly bearing giant cucumbers or dahlias, we each appeared grasping some impressive-looking part of our submission. The Minister congratulated us on our entre-preneurial spirit. Broackes said that he would never regret the experience, even if he did not win. James Sherwood beamed. The rest of us complimented him on the way he had avoided any disclosure of his project until the day of the submission. It had come as a great surprise. We each displayed as much *bonhomie* as we could muster.

The next stage in the proceedings was the photo-opportunity. For this we crowded into a small room full of cameramen, to be photographed first singly with Ridley as we handed him our proposal, and then collectively like a row of school prefects with the headmaster.

We also had our own press launch at the Inn on the Park Hotel. We offered champagne and sausages over breakfast; and we distributed copies of the summary and showed the up-to-date video. Emphasizing the joint nature of our enterprise, I said that the French, who had always specialized in imaginative projects of this kind – they had, after all, pioneered both the Suez and Panama Canals – had by the 1970s become the world's expert in transportation systems. I presented to the audience the senior members of the CTG team and the directors, calling upon each in turn to take a bow like performers in a pop group. Finally, I managed to invoke Shakespeare in our cause, saying that he had described life as a shuttle.

With the transmission of our projects we felt we were past an important landmark; I am not sure that any of us realized the scuffle that was to follow in the next few weeks.

The Mandate

Although control had now been handed over to the two Governments this did not, as it turned out, mean that we, the proposers, could take a back seat and simply await their judgement. The next two and a half months leading up to the decision of 20 January 1986 were to prove as busy as the pre-submission phase – and much more tense. We became involved in a dialogue with the Governments; and there was considerable manoeuvring between the organizations left in the field. On a quite different plane we also had to tune our public relations to reach a climax at the crucial moment of ministerial decision.

For a long time CTG had been trying to conclude an agreement about the use that the railways would make of the tunnel and the revenue we could expect to receive. This was not easy, given the uncertainty about likely traffic needs in the mid-1990s and the involvement of four parties – France Manche, British Rail, SNCF and ourselves. Not long after we had put in our submission I received a message from Nicholas Ridley that anybody who hoped to gain the mandate must provide the Governments with the details of a hard-and-fast agreement about the traffic and tariffs to be derived from railway usage. It was impossible for Ridley to assess the financial viability of any scheme unless he had clear-cut details of revenue figures for rail. If such information was not provided by the end of November the whole timetable for the decision on the link might be in jeopardy. Our submission had contained estimates about rail revenue for passengers and freight which represented a large proportion of our income. What the Government now wanted was something to show categorically that the sort of assumptions we were working on would be acceptable to the railway companies.

We, the would-be operators on the one side and the railways on the other, approached the subject from such different angles that it was several weeks before we could reach even heads of agreement on principles. Helped by our consultants, Wilbur Smith and Setec Economie, we tried to estimate tariffs, taking account of likely tolls for other cross-Channel traffic at the time. British Rail, however, wished to determine them on the basis of the return required to meet increased capital costs, resulting from the tunnel link. There was a particular difficulty on the French side. SNCF gave the impression then, and later, that they wanted to become part managers or even part owners of the project because they saw the financial advantages to be gained from it. They therefore stalled until pressurized from on high by the French Government. Thanks to the ingenuity and doggedness of Martin Hemingway, a long-standing member of the Hammersmith team, who remained on the footplate throughout our rail negotiations, we just managed to patch up an understanding that tided us over this particular difficulty, but it did not prevent us running into a battalion of sorrows at a later stage when we had to proceed to heads of agreement and then a detailed agreement on rail revenue.

I was worried that some people in Government were afraid that our project would lead to trade union disruption and domination. It was suggested to me that we were going to be dependent upon the co-operation of the British railway unions – NUR (the National Union of Railwaymen) and ASLEF (the Associated Society of Locomotive Engineers and Firemen). As I explained in two letters to Ridley, this was not our intention at all. The shuttle would be run by us, not by British Rail. We were going to recruit and run our own labour force. We foresaw the need to introduce special terms and conditions appropriate to the relatively small scale and continuous nature of our operations. We had already had instructive discussions with the unions on the subject of the through rail service.

The last-minute entry into the lists of James Sherwood's project, Expressway, captured the headlines and caused us a lot of anxiety. When first submitted, the Expressway scheme seemed to provide for tunnels to be used by both vehicles and trains, ventilation and fresh air to be furnished by two ventilation shafts and by specially designed electrostatic precipitators.[7] However, Sherwood subsequently indicated that they might have separate tunnels for trains and road traffic. The weaknesses of the project were that there was no French partner (the French assessment team also objected to the way Sherwood had been allowed to change his project after the closing date for applications); and there was no clear indication of where the money was to come from. The total capacity would be half that of ours. We, in CTG, also thought that the Expressway scheme created serious difficulties for drivers and ventilation. The former might be a matter for speculation. But we had done enough research on tunnel ventilation to know that, on the basis of current technology and without spending exorbitant sums, the exhaust problem created by vehicles in a tunnel such as Sherwood proposed could not adequately be dealt with. It was surprising to us that the British Government did not seem to share these doubts, either about driver disorientation or about ventilation. They seemed to presume, somewhat supinely we thought, that drivers would be able to drive twenty miles in a tunnel without undue anxiety, and that, despite the risks of accident and fire, traffic would keep moving and so remove all danger of a build-up of fumes from vehicle emissions. One doubt the Government did seem to accept was whether, given the large diameter of Sherwood's proposed tunnels, they would be able to fit into the chalk layer beneath the sea bed of the Channel.

Certainly the Expressway scheme had attractive features. Sherwood said that his costs of construction were going to be half ours. He could also claim the advantages of a drive-through. Not least important, he himself was an engaging personality who had shown himself to be a dynamic entrepreneur.

From the day it was launched, Expressway caused special worry to the French, not so much because they thought it feasible but because they thought the British Government did. The French authorities had wished to eliminate Expressway at the start but Ridley resisted this. Indeed our French partners were convinced that he favoured the scheme, or that at any rate he would urge any promoter who wanted to secure the mandate to get together with Sherwood. I am sure that Sherwood did have supporters in the British camp. He also had detractors. Indeed there was a conflict of view about him and his scheme, which was one of the reasons why it was so difficult for those of us outside the magic Whitehall circle to know what the outcome would be.

At about the same time as we were getting this strong lead from Paris about the popularity in London of Expressway, the other main cross-Channel ferry operator, European Ferries, had publicized their readiness to join whichever group secured the mandate. So if we were going to have to join up with an existing ferry operator, as some people were suggesting we should, we

[7] These produce electric charges which remove solid particles like smoke from the air, but not noxious gases like carbon monoxide.

would have to consider European Ferries as well as Sherwood's Sealink. From the talks I had with various people in London I concluded that the Minister of Transport was certainly looking at the Sherwood scheme seriously; after all he was the only ferry operator to have submitted a proposal. Ridley is difficult to interpret, embodying as he does the instincts of an artist, the training of an engineer and the profession of a politician. This complicated make-up has been compounded by the philosophy he says he acquired at the Foreign Office when he was Minister there. He learned from the Foreign Office that it is necessary in any complex negotiation to begin by persuading all the protagonists that it is likely to fail. This means suggesting confusion in your own mind as well. You tell everyone that they have lost and then ask whether it might be possible to rescue something from the wreck. In that way you can establish the bottom line of all parties involved. Then you can start negotiating again, this time seriously.[8] This is how Ridley described what he learned from the Foreign Office, and, as you read it, you must admit that the Foreign Office is a school for scandal.

Ridley was evidently anxious that, when the Channel link came before Ministers for a decision, they should have before them a number of plausible alternatives, not simply be asked to approve one applicant. How far he himself favoured Sherwood's scheme for this tactical purpose, or whether he wanted it there to help him exert leverage on other proposers, or whether he really believed in it – these were questions I found it difficult to answer – as I think did Ridley's officials, who were, however, impeccably discreet. There is no doubt that Sherwood had influence in high places in London. He was also always supremely confident that he was going to win.

However, on the basis of what I discovered, the strong advice I gave to the members of our own Board and to our French partners was that we should stick to our plan, remain calm and avoid running after any other proposer. There was no need for us to join up with anyone else. We would be judged on our own merits.

Parliamentary discussion on the link took place towards the end of the year, culminating in debates in the House of Commons on 9 December 1985 and in the House of Lords on the 13th. We had a close shave in the Transport Committee of the House of Commons when it needed the casting vote of the chairman to produce a verdict in favour of our scheme. In the frequent appearances that members of our team had to make before Committees of both Houses of Parliament the gap between the political and business worlds opened starkly before me, the latter being more mystified by the politicians than the other way round. I could not help noticing by contrast how relatively little attention our French partners had to pay to the enquiries and pressures

[8] Interview with Malcolm Rutherford, *Financial Times*, 24 January 1986.

of the Chamber of Deputies, which reflected not merely the lesser political interest aroused by the subject in France but the difference in our systems of government. The House of Lords debate was characterized by the number of peers who had to declare their interest for one scheme or the other.

Rabies continued high on the public's indignation hit list. A correspondent wrote to the *Yorkshire Evening Press* as follows:

> By agreeing to a Channel Tunnel Mrs Thatcher is leaving this country wide open to a real threat of rabies when the French rats have a free run to our land.

Explaining that he was not just ventilating a personal view but reflecting the interests of many organizations, the Duke of Wellington wrote to me expressing concern at the risks of rabies, foot and mouth and other diseases entering Britain. I replied to him as follows:

> We have had very extensive discussions with the Ministry of Agriculture, Fisheries and Food, and veterinary and rabies experts on all these matters. Very stringent precautions will be taken to prevent the unauthorized entry of any animals into Britain and, with respect to the risk of rabid animals getting into the tunnel, the most important line of defence is to prevent any litter, waste or toilet discharge in the tunnel by the use of sealed toilets and windows on all trains or shuttles passing through the tunnel. This will significantly reduce the attraction of the tunnel as a possible source of food to such animals. Secondly, the entry to the tunnel and terminal will have several lines of fences proofed against animals, together with detection equipment, which, we believe, will be more than adequate to prevent such animals from entering Britain by that means. Unfortunately, all the indications are that the much greater risk occurs through people bringing in animals in their cars or on small boats crossing the Channel.

As my contribution at this time to the quickening of the dance and the shuffling of the partners I invited Nigel Broackes to lunch. It was a return, a belated return, for the hospitality he had offered me in February. We talked with the usual frankness about our projects and our prospects, but, as before, it was apparent that there was no advantage for CTG in the sort of merger Broackes still hankered after.

Another event that sticks in my memory from this stage, because it was such an anticlimax, was the meeting France Manche and CTG had with the French and British assessment teams. This took place in London on 11 December. The purpose was not to cross-examine us on our proposal but to clarify certain things that might arise if we were awarded the mandate, for example the length of the concession period. I think that we and our French partners were reassured by the meeting; such questioning as had occurred was not hostile at all and could be regarded as a sign of serious interest and preparation for possible concession negotiations. If it was, as I say, an anticlimax this was because we were far from complacent about our prospects, and, brainwashed by the hostile press, we had been hesitant to persuade ourselves that our project was so well worked out that it left few questions to be answered.

I had lunch once again with Mrs Thatcher on Boxing Day (1985), but we both avoided the subject, except that she said, crossing her fingers and holding them before me, 'I'm sure you're doing this.' By the turn of the year Ministers were moving into the fast lane. I had always feared that they might be tempted to fudge a decision and end up by urging two or more of the promoters to get together; but I had been assured repeatedly that they would not do this. The mandate would be clear-cut and awarded to one of the contenders. All the same, both Governments were subjected to heavy pressures, even though conflicting ones. Officials in both countries and the joint assessment team had expressed their views but inevitably it was up to Ministers to reach a decision.

My French opposite number told me of the meeting of the French and British Ministers of Transport on 7 January 1986. They had played the game of eliminations. Of the four contenders for the mandate they had agreed to eliminate the bridge proposal without much difficulty. Jean Auroux had then suggested the elimination of Sherwood's Expressway scheme on the grounds that it had no adequate French participation and that it had not been worked out properly from the point of view either of finance or of technology. Nicholas Ridley contested this, arguing that there were certain important advantages in the Expressway scheme, particularly the idea of a drive-through. He went on to say that he favoured the elimination of Euroroute. The British Government did not think that the mixed scheme for bridges and a tube on the seabed was feasible, but Auroux was not prepared to accept this – Euroroute had for long been the favourite of the French Government; and it certainly had a powerful list of French backers. Apparently the discussion about these two schemes continued for some time and there was practically no talk about the Channel Tunnel Group Scheme.

Jean-Paul Parayre came to London and gave me this graphic account early on 8 January 1986. We were to have a meeting of our joint Board later that morning and Ridley had asked to see me in the afternoon. Parayre and I discussed tactics. Evidently it was necessary, as this final hand was being played, to devise some way of ruffing the drive-through ace held by our opponents. I suggested to Parayre that I should inform the Ministry of Transport immediately at the official level that the Channel Tunnel Group and France Manche were prepared to give an undertaking now that, should the traffic grow and the technology permit, we would be ready to consider a drive-through at some stage. Parayre was enthusiastic about this because the French side were convinced of the attachment of the British Government to a drive-through. I thereupon spoke to the Ministry of Transport and conveyed this undertaking.

Unfortunately my message was misunderstood and the Minister apparently gained the impression that we were prepared to join Expressway, which was not our intention at all. This misunderstanding may have been at the root of the line that Ridley took with me in the afternoon. He said that the British Government would, if possible, like a drive-through and a rail-through. He wondered, therefore, whether the Channel Tunnel Group and France Manche would be prepared to make an approach to Sherwood with a view to joining the Expressway scheme. I said that my first reaction to this was that from the point of view of organization we had no reason whatever to join up with Sherwood. Neither he nor his organization had anything to offer us; we had all the experience, technology and finance that was necessary to build any sort of link including, if necessary, a drive-through. As regards this last idea we had considered the possibility of a drive-through last spring in great detail and had come to the conclusion that it was not a valid proposition in present circumstances. The problems of construction had not been solved; nor had those of ventilation. We did not therefore believe that it would be possible to raise the money at this stage for a drive-through. Nevertheless I could assure him that after we had had experience of tunnelling under the Channel with our much smaller tunnels, and if the technological and financial circumstances changed in favour of a drive-through, we would be prepared to undertake such a scheme.

Ridley continued to suggest that we should join up with Sherwood. I said that he had nothing to offer that we could not provide. Ridley replied that he had a drive-through to offer. I answered that we would provide a drive-through if circumstances permitted. Upon which Ridley said that he thought we were in danger of repeating ourselves. It was left that I would consult the Channel Tunnel Group Board and our French partners and get back to him, with an answer to his proposition.

Ridley revealed to me that he had already received Sherwood and would be seeing Broackes. Before many hours had elapsed Sherwood was putting it out to the press that he was going to get the mandate and that other people would be wishing to join up with him. I authorized a public statement that we had no intention of joining up with Expressway.

I spent a lot of time in the next two days trying to get across to British Ministers what it was that we were prepared to undertake. In my clarifications

I included No. 10, where I discovered that the Prime Minister, like most other Ministers, had been given the false impression that we were prepared to join up with Expressway. Stuck in the traffic in Holborn one midday, my car telephone rang. It was Ridley. Insouciant as ever, despite the pressure, he sought some further explanation, which I gave him to the sound of hooting. During these days I also attempted to discover whether and why Sherwood really had the inside track as he was claiming. It seemed to me odd that he should apparently be so favoured. He was a ferry operator who initially had been against any idea of a fixed link; indeed he was a member of Flexilink, an organization whose purpose was to oppose the creation of any fixed link. He had only put in an offer for a fixed link at a very late stage. As I have mentioned, the original scheme, which just got in under the wire on 31 October, involved two large tunnels which would be used by both rail and vehicles. When it was pointed out to him that this would be quite unacceptable he shifted his scheme to the building of two twelve-metre tunnels for vehicle traffic and two smaller tunnels for rail. We pointed out to the Ministry of Transport that in allowing Sherwood to alter his scheme after the deadline of 31 October, they were doing what was tantamount to moving the goal posts – Cliff Chetwood's favourite phrase. But they told us that we would be wise to overlook this.

On 9 January we had a Board meeting of the Channel Tunnel Group, at which I told the directors of Ridley's proposition. They reacted indignantly. They said there was no case for joining up with Sherwood or accepting the idea of a drive-through now. I had some difficulty in persuading them that I thought that we would have to undertake to build a drive-through in certain circumstances. They were opposed to this but I persuaded them that we would be able to work out a form of words that would show flexibility without involving a dangerous commitment. Reluctantly they accepted this and suggested that two of their number, namely Denis Child of National Westminster and Terrel Wyatt of the construction company, Costain, should accompany me when I next saw the Minister. This appointment was arranged during the Board meeting and we agreed to go along and see Ridley again at nine o'clock the next morning, that is to say on Friday, 10 January.

Following the Board meeting and after telephone conversations with Parayre, who had meanwhile returned to Paris, I spent a lot of time drafting a reply to Ridley. In this I wanted to include material about construction and ventilation problems of a drive-through; so we had quite a team from Hammersmith helping in the drafting. We did this in a lengthy drafting session at Suffolk Street, helped by bottles of white wine from the bar opposite. During the course of the night I managed to get the text to Parayre and he rang me up at eight o'clock the following morning to say that he agreed with it. When, accompanied by Child and Wyatt, I met Ridley, he was in a benign mood. I told him of our attitude and gave him a letter. This stated categorically that we could not enter into a joint proposal for a scheme such as that put forward by Expressway. It outlined the research we had done into a drive-through and the technical problems in present circumstances of construction, ventilation, driver psychology and safety. We gave an assurance about the capacity and speed of our shuttle for the transport of vehicles. Finally the letter contained the following commitment about a drive-through:

> It is difficult at the moment to be categorical about the scale upon which traffic is going to develop; however, if the traffic warrants it, if there is a demand for a drive-through and if the various problems and uncertainties of a drive-through, referred to above, can be met in a way compatible with market financing, Channel Tunnel Group and France Manche will be prepared to develop and implement a drive-through tunnel as an expansion of our scheme.

Ridley explained that the British Government wanted something more, so that at a later stage they could not be accused of having limited the amount of capacity across the Channel to something below what the public wanted. We pointed out that we had to have exclusive rights for a certain period of time or we would not be able to raise the money. In the end we undertook to try to produce a formula that would insure against any artificial limitation of link capacity. I wrote to Ridley again on 13 January giving him such a formula.

The press was full of speculation about the readiness of Sherwood and Broackes to get together. Over the coming weekend I had several conversations with Parayre about the varying intriguing combinations. He told me that Bouygues had been in Britain on 10 January, when he had seen Broackes and Sherwood separately. Bouygues had been there privately and not on behalf of France Manche. Subsequently I learned that he had suggested to Sherwood as a personal idea, perhaps worth considering, that there might be a carve-up: Euroroute would undertake the finance, CTG–FM would do the construction and he, Sherwood, would be the operator. It was not clear which of the various schemes was to be implemented but Bouygues' idea seemed to be that that the Governments should choose the three of us and we three would then decide which project to implement.

Monday, 13 January started hectically with the telephones bringing reports of offers and deals by and between various proposers. The two Ministers of Transport were due to meet that morning in London and they were expected to reach a joint view on whom to recommend to their governments as the winner of the beauty contest. Mrs Thatcher and the French President were going to meet in Lille on 20 January to announce the decision. Parayre rang me early on the 13th to report on various accounts he had received of what Auroux would be proposing and how the French saw the attitude of the British Government. Later he telephoned again to say that he would be coming to London immediately to be on hand should one or both Ministers wish to see us.

Immediately after his telephone call I rang the Ministry of Transport to find out whether Ridley or the two Ministers might be wishing to talk with us later that day. I also talked about the beauty contest. The senior official with whom I spoke repeated several times that the decision was completely open and he would not like to bet who was going to win.

As the morning wore on and the telephone calls became more frantic I was given a message from Bouygues' representative in London, John Stansby, that Broackes was inviting Parayre and me to lunch that day at the Ritz. I replied that I could not commit Parayre because he was coming over to see me and I was planning to give him lunch. Stansby was speaking to me on the telephone from his car and he revealed that he was going to the airport to meet Parayre. The latter would take any orders he got from Bouygues and if Bouygues said that we should lunch with Broackes we would have to do so. I said that I thought that the only thing to do was to get Parayre to ring me as soon as he arrived at the airport and then we would decide together whether or not to lunch with Broackes. Parayre rang me and in the end we did decide to accept Broackes's invitation, though Parayre said that he was not subject to Bouygues' orders. He came to Suffolk Street first and we had a short chat about the fluctuating scene before going on to lunch.

The Broackes lunch party in the Trafalgar Suite of the Ritz was not at all what we had been led to expect. Instead of a small gathering of just us three and one or two others, Broackes introduced us to the entire board of Trafalgar House saying it had been a happy coincidence that they were due to lunch together that day anyway. In the course of lunch Broackes said that he was not at all interested in the Expressway scheme, which he considered to be quite impracticable. He floated once again the idea to us that we should have an arrangement together by which Euroroute would build their bridges and immersed tube for vehicles and we would build a tunnel for rail traffic. Parayre, backed up by me, explained why this was no good from our point of view. Parayre went on to say that although there could be no acceptance by us of the Euroroute scheme, we had an open mind about personnel and did not want to exclude the possibility of bringing people in from other projects.

Broackes went on to say that he had submitted a considerable modification of his scheme to Ridley. He had suggested that if there were difficulties from the point of view of security or environment in having a bridge and spiral on the British side he would be prepared to consider dispensing with that and running the immersed tube from the Kent coast out to the island on the French side. I was as sure that the British authorities had strong objections on security grounds to Euroroute's scheme as I was that this device would not satisfy them.

Tuesday, 14 January was spent in negotiating texts. The Ministry of Transport insisted that they were carrying out the same sort of negotiation with the two other contenders left in the field (the bridge scheme had been tacitly rejected) and that the fact that they were doing so with us should not be taken as any indication that we had been chosen. I became used to hearing this reservation and found that it saved a lot of time if I introduced it myself at the beginning of any conversation with officials. The subject of much discussion that day and for the rest of the week was the terms of the understanding with the Governments about our readiness in certain circumstances to construct a drive-through. It had become increasingly apparent to me the previous week that unless we could offer categorically now to consider a drive-through if technology and traffic permitted we would be excluded. Both British and French Governments needed a drive-through. They thought that they would be accused of being old-fashioned and of not coping with the twenty-first century if a drive-through was not included in the project chosen. Indeed Parayre at the beginning of the week was saying that Mitterrand definitely favoured Euroroute because it was the more grandiose scheme and because it had a drive-through. Ridley had never left me in any doubt that he wanted a drive-through. I was therefore quite convinced that we had to hold out the prospect of a drive-through as agreed by our Board the previous week. I wrote to the Prime Minister accordingly.

Although, during the next day or two, I was in constant touch with officials at the Ministry of Transport, I had difficulty in reading the Minister's own mind and in deciding what else we would have to do to persuade him to recommend our project for the mandate. There was no doubt that he was going to run into a lot of trouble from those of the applicants who were turned down. I was told that in some way we ought to be ready to compensate Broackes, if he was rejected, for the cost he had incurred in making his submission. At times I felt that it would be a *sine qua non* for us to bring in either Sherwood or Broackes if we were to get the mandate. I explained all this frequently on the telephone to Parayre who was reasonably, but only reasonably, tolerant on hearing it. He said that, without wishing to be accused of I-told-you-so-ism, he had frequently reminded me how beholden some members of the British Government seemed to be to Sherwood.

We had a meeting of our Board on 15 January, when I told the directors that the outcome was still uncertain. I had been warned many times that we could not assume that we were the winners. We discussed whether there was any way we could – or indeed if we should – help Ministers face the music from those who were rejected. I cannot say that the withers of our Board members were wrung by the prospect of the trouble Ministers might run into for saying no to either Broackes or Sherwood. I said that I had received an invitation from Sherwood to lunch the following day, so I needed to know what line they wanted me to take. Without any prevarication they said that they were not prepared to give any undertaking to either Sherwood or Broackes. They recognized that if we could incorporate one or other into our scheme it would enhance our prospects of getting the mandate and make things easier for the Governments. But they did not think that we could compromise on the project; there was no need to bring in either of the other contestants; and they saw no reason to panic about our prospects.

We then had a long discussion about publicity, a subject which always led to interminable argument. This time we were confronted with strong pressure from the banks to insert advertisements in the press in such a way as to influence Ministers before the Cabinet meeting due to take place on the following day, 16 January. The cost of such advertisements would be of the order of £70,000. I am glad to say that, eloquently briefed by Bill Shakespeare, we decided against doing so. I was able to tell the directors that I had just written to all the members of the Cabinet setting out the central features of our scheme, beginning with our readiness to build a drive-through in certain circumstances. The text of the letter of 15 January was read out at the meeting and the Board members seemed pleased with it.

I lunched with James Sherwood on Thursday, 16 January in his impressive Sea Container offices near Blackfriars Bridge. There was nobody else present. Sherwood said that the Department of Transport had indicated a wish for him to get into touch with me. According to his information Broackes had been told by Ridley that his scheme was no longer a runner. That left Expressway and CTG alone in the field. Sherwood described the personal proposal Bouygues had put to him the previous Friday, which he had told Bouygues he would think about. This he had done over the weekend and had replied on Monday the 13th on the following lines: that CTG and Expressway should begin by constructing a single-rail, seven-metre tunnel from the French coast. This would enable them to see what tunnelling conditions were like beneath the Channel. On the strength of the experience gained they would then be able to decide whether to go ahead with the idea of two drive-through bored tunnels, or to stick to the existing CTG–FM idea of rail tunnels with through trains and the shuttle. Sherwood indicated that he had discussed this idea with the Ministry of Transport, who were not against him putting it to CTG.

We had considerable discussion about the practicality in present circumstances of contemplating large bored drive-through tunnels. Sherwood admitted that his capacity would be limited at the moment to 1,600 vehicles per hour each way (i.e. half that of our scheme), but he was confident that this could be considerably increased. He said Ridley had told him that he was completely satisfied with the ventilation aspect of the Expressway scheme. I replied that I was surprised to hear this because the Japanese proposal for electrostatic precipitators did not deal with the difficulty of carbon monoxide. Sherwood said that his Japanese adviser had told him that their scheme was perfectly adequate for this and the British Ministry of Transport had accepted such a verdict, although they admitted that there might be difficulties in the event of some accident. I told Sherwood of the specialist studies that we and the French had carried out last year which concluded that ventilation and construction of a drive-through tunnel were not practical or financially feasible in present circumstances.

Returning to the counter-proposal that Sherwood had put to Bouygues, I said that a project of this kind would inevitably involve the postponement of operations. If you were starting with just a single rail tunnel obviously the date when any throughput of vehicles could start would be delayed, thereby affecting the financing of the scheme. Sherwood said that it would certainly be delayed by one year. I also spoke about the difficulty of raising money for so uncertain a scheme. I added that simply by boring one seven-metre tunnel you would scarcely be able to come to a conclusion about the feasibility of a much wider tunnel that would have to be bored in two different substances, the gault (predominantly clay) as well as the chalk. Nor did I think that in the space of time he was talking about, namely the next two years or so, technology was likely to have improved to such an extent as to meet the ventilation and other problems of a twenty-mile drive-through. Our discussion ended by my repeating all our doubts about anything in the nature of a drive-through at this stage; however, in order to get off Sherwood's hook, I undertook to get into touch with Bouygues to find out his reaction to the proposal that Sherwood had put to him. Sherwood expressed some fear that this might lead to the creation of bad blood and I said that I would avoid this. In fact I said nothing to Bouygues; there was no point when we were in the final furlong.

Sherwood obviously believed that he had made a considerable impact on Ridley. The line he had taken with Ridley was that any fixed link would inevitably put out of business the existing ferries in the Channel; and that the CTG shuttle scheme would not provide a sufficiently advanced service to justify this. Evidently Sherwood thought that Ridley, much impressed by this line of argument, was eager that the two of us should get together.

At about the same time, on Thursday, 16 January, when Sherwood and I were starting lunch, the Cabinet must have broken up after reaching their decision on the mandate. Naturally, like everyone else involved, I was eager to learn the outcome but all I managed to discover was that the Government, despite all the merger pressures that had been exercised, were going to stick by their original promise to come down clearly in favour of one project rather than try to organize some amalgam.

Following the Cabinet meeting, Ridley flew to Paris to see Auroux on Thursday afternoon. Speculation came to a head by about midnight when it was reported that they had reached agreement. No details were given. I received what I thought was a favourable indicator on Thursday evening. I had a telephone call from Sir Geoffrey Howe. Some weeks earlier we had been invited to spend the coming weekend with the Howes at Chevening. Howe told me on the telephone that he was overcome with embarrassment and hoped that I would forgive him but when he had invited us he had completely forgotten that it would be just ahead of the summit meeting at Lille on the 20th to which he would be accompanying the Prime Minister. He thought it would be awkward if it came out afterwards that I had spent the weekend with him. I told him that of course I understood and I hoped we could come another time. In fact the postponement gave me considerable encouragement because I deduced – not that it required a blinding flash of imagination – that if it had been decided by the Cabinet that we were not the winners, then there would be no particular embarrassment to Howe or others if it came out that we had spent the weekend with the Foreign Secretary.

All Friday was spent on different aspects of negotiation, largely to provide for our readiness at some stage to build a drive-through. The Governments were very keen to have this incorporated in their declared decision. Just to show how near to the cliff-edge we were I should record that the formula for a drive-through was only finally agreed – between Melville Guest and Andrew Lyall – at lunchtime on Sunday, 19 January, less than twenty-four hours before the Heads of Government were due to meet.

The Government insisted that they were continuing to carry out similar negotiations with the other promoters on various aspects of the concession and that negotiating with us should not be taken to imply anything. However, the greater the detail on which we negotiated during the course of a long day, the more I came to the view that this must be a good sign. Because if we had been rejected they would have been much tougher in negotiating these details of the concessions on the grounds that it would not much matter to them if their terms were unacceptable to us.

On Saturday, 18 January, the press were full of the subject. There was a report on the front page of *The Times* of an interview with Nigel Broackes in which he was severely critical of Ridley for showing favouritism to Sherwood. It was true that at the end of the interview he said that the project that 'Sir Nicholas Henderson has come forward with at the last minute of a drive-through is preposterous', but that did us no harm; what did us good in the public eye was for the two tycoons to be quarrelling and for one to be accusing Ridley of favouring the other.

I was at Suffolk Street on Saturday morning, dealing with last-minute hold-ups on rail tariffs and on the manner in which our commitment about a drive-through could be announced. The terms of the latter were published subsequently in a White Paper.[9] Later at home I was in telephonic touch with the Department of Transport and something that was said to me left me in no doubt that we were the winners. However, it was not of a category that enabled me to say anything or to reveal that I knew.

Tough negotiations continued throughout Saturday and Sunday and during much of the nights. They were difficult largely because of the problems SNCF were creating about a rail agreement. I had a telephone call in the middle of the night of 19/20 January from Parayre saying that he was in a state of considerable despair about the failure to reach agreement with SNCF. Auroux, the French Minister of Transport, had just told him that what was happening, or not happening, was disastrous. I said that there was nothing I could do at that stage; we had reached an agreement with British Rail which was all that the British Government required. Auroux had apparently also expressed indignation at the line the Sunday press in Britain had been taking. They had jumped the gun in reporting that a decision had been taken in favour of CTG–FM. This was not true: no decision would be taken until Mitterrand and the Prime Minister met. Then at midnight on Sunday Colin Stannard rang up. He was leading our delegation in Paris, trying to tie up an understanding on railways with SNCF, but he reported that they had failed to reach agreement. They were all in a state of great anxiety. I repeated what I had told Parayre, that on the basis of my information the British Government believed that there was a satisfactory agreement between British Rail and us.

We were on tenterhooks throughout the final days before the Heads of Government meeting at Lille on Monday, 20 January. I noticed how wary people in Government were of being seen talking to me, as if I was some bacillus. Once more, I took this to be a good sign, as well as yet one more indicator of the gulf between the public and private sectors.

I went to sleep on Sunday night, or early Monday morning, in a state of fair but not total confidence. A terrible gale had blown up and I wondered whether the Prime Minister would succeed in flying to Lille to meet the French President as arranged. Any delay, I realized, could jeopardize the whole thing. However, all went well with the Lille flight. Neither Parayre nor I had been invited to attend the ceremony; our joint team was represented, but very nervously on the French side. When the French representatives, led by Jean Renault, arrived at Lille they were entirely unconvinced that we had secured

---

[9] Command 9735, February 1986.

the mandate. I think it was the only occasion when British sang-froid really showed itself – maybe because it was based on better intelligence. I went to Suffolk Street early on Monday morning. There were plenty of television cameras on the doorstep. It was not until I heard the speeches from Lille on the radio around noon that I knew everything had gone through satisfactorily. The rest of the day was a long series of telephone calls and press and television conferences. In the afternoon I listened to Ridley making a statement in the House of Commons and then answering questions. What was interesting to me was the lack of enthusiasm for the project on both sides of the House. Most of the Tories who spoke were representing constituents in some way adversely affected by the idea of a fixed link. On the Opposition benches there had been no decision to come out in favour of the fixed link so the most vociferous speakers were the traditional anti-Europeans who were against the whole thing. However, I was somewhat encouraged by the fact that nobody criticized Ridley for having chosen us rather than one of the others.

Ridley wrote to me on 20 January to let me 'know officially that the Prime Minister and the French President announced this morning in Lille that the Governments of the two countries have agreed to take together the necessary steps to facilitate the development, construction and operation of a Fixed Link across the Channel by the Channel Tunnel Group'. He added: 'This is a historic decision. There is much to be done to carry it forward to a successful outcome, but I am confident that with effort and co-operation we can succeed.'

I replied in a similarly confident but uneuphoric vein.

I have often been asked, and asked myself, why we were chosen. With remarkable frankness the British Government published the joint Anglo-French assessment in a White Paper.[10] This showed that they had decided in favour of our project for the following reasons:

(1) it was the soundest financially;
(2) it carried the fewest technical risks;
(3) it was safest from the traveller's point of view;
(4) it presented no maritime problem;
(5) it was the least vulnerable to sabotage and terrorist action;
(6) it had an environmental impact that could be contained.

As I have already said, our project was financially the most robust and this gave us a great advantage. Our initial weakness was that our submission made no reference to a drive-through. We were fortunate in the timing of our subsequent commitment on this. Had we given an undertaking earlier

---

[10] Command 9735.

that we would promise to build a drive-through, our competitors might well have over-trumped us. As it was, we came forward with the idea at the key moment when Ministers were on the point of reaching a decision. Without this undertaking I am not at all sure that we would have secured the mandate; I am certain that we would not have won exclusive rights to last until the year 2020. As regards timing, I have learned subsequently that the French Government sent an emissary over to see Sir Robert Armstrong at a crucial point to make it clear that, although President Mitterrand favoured Euroroute, he would probably be prepared to set this preference aside and go for CTG–FM; but he could not withdraw his support for Euroroute so long as the British Government maintained its support for Expressway. This was the ultimate in the process of eliminations.

But I would not wish to leave it simply on that negative note. It would be wrong, I think, to conclude that our proposal was a second-best choice, decided upon as the one to which both sides had the least objections. The second-best syndrome was partly the fault of both Governments. They had done so much to talk up the number of good horses in the field, those carrying drive-through being by no means the least favoured, that when CTG–FM were signalled as first past the finishing post, the result was seen as something of a let-down – the idea of a drive-through having been proposed by us for a later stage. Our scheme, however, was one that both Governments recognized as corresponding to the needs and hopes, political and economic, of Britain, of France and of Western Europe generally. 'Today's decision', Mrs Thatcher said after the issue of the joint communiqué at Lille on 20 January, 'is a dramatic step in Anglo-French co-operation. The project we have agreed upon will have immense significance for trade and communications between our two countries. It is also important for the enormous opportunity we are giving to the private sector to demonstrate their abilities and their enterprise in a project of the utmost public importance.'

Although it is chronologically outside the scope of this account, I must record here that when, in the summer of 1986, the subject was discussed in Parliament at Second Reading and in Select Committee there was a remarkable degree of all-party support for the CTG project. Any other choice would certainly have created much greater parliamentary difficulty as well as running into more objections from environmentalists. The fact that we included rail-through for passengers and freight was seen as encouraging the shifting of traffic off the roads. A drive-through was promised when circumstances permitted. Meanwhile the rolling road of a shuttle would provide a quick and reliable means for vehicular traffic. Whether the verdict of the French and British Governments is vindicated will depend on the quality of service provided by the tunnel for both trains and vehicles over the next three decades.

Personal Conclusion

I had always said that my chairmanship would be temporary; the granting of the mandate seemed a good moment to go. But I stayed on for the conclusion of the Anglo-French Treaty signed by President Mitterrand and Mrs Thatcher at Canterbury on 12 February 1986. Jean-Paul Parayre and I, as well as other members of our Groups, were asked to attend the ceremony, which we did like beaters invited by the landlords to observe the bag after a successful day's shooting. I also waited to leave until the end of the protracted negotiations on the concession. This was signed by Jean Auroux and Nicholas Ridley and by Jean-Paul Parayre and myself on 14 March 1986. With the coming into force of the concession agreement France Manche and the Channel Tunnel Group became merged in a single organization, Eurotunnel. This organization became responsible for carrying out the biggest private industrial project of the twentieth century. After the concession agreement was signed I handed over to Lord Pennock. In one sense, because it gave me time for other things, I was relieved to give up one of the most difficult tasks I have undertaken, yet I was immensely pleased to have taken part in such an unusual experience involving business and government, French and English. I remain totally committed to the idea of the Channel-tunnel link and I have been appointed to the joint Eurotunnel Board. We will traverse many difficult times before we go through the tunnel by train or shuttle. I am as sure of the recurrence of frequent crises as I am of the ultimate successful completion of the project.

The Channel Tunnel Group

Members	Representative on CTG Board
Balfour Beatty	D. A. Holland
Costain	J. Reeve, succeeded by T. Wyatt
Tarmac	A. Osborne
Taylor Woodrow	F. R. Gibb
George Wimpey	A. McDowall, succeeded by C. J. Chetwood
National Westminster Bank	D. M. Child
Midland Bank	I. Paterson

Merchant bank advisers: Morgan Grenfell (represented by J. Franklin) and Robert Fleming (represented by C. Moore).

The CTG began as an informal group. On 26 April 1985 the company, The Channel Tunnel Group Ltd, was incorporated with a share capital of £7, issued as a £1 share to each member.

DIFFERENT APPROACHES TO FOREIGN POLICY

*Lecture to the Department of War Studies,
King's College, London, 13 May 1986.*

Different Approaches to Foreign Policy

I want to speak to you today about three of the countries in which I have worked, the Federal Republic of Germany, France and the United States – about their different approaches to foreign policy in the post-war world, distinctions that arise in part from their varied geographical situation and in part from their contrasted histories. I am not going to discuss varying diplomatic techniques or methods; and you need have no fear that I am about to deliver a lecture on diplomatic history. I swear I am not going to talk about 'perceptions' – that word used with such abandon in foreign policy analysis. What I am going to do is to pick out certain things in the attitude of those countries to the outside world that have struck me.

All countries, in the conduct of their foreign relations, are affected by their past, but none more so than West Germany. Comparing his country with others, Helmut Schmidt has said that 'Germany is set apart by its past.' Yet, in some ways, I found the Germans' attitude on this subject strange. When, for instance, some fourteen years ago now, I first arrived in Bonn, having come from Poland, a very senior member of the German Government told me that he could not see why the Poles continued to bear a grudge against the Germans because the Germans felt no grievance against the Poles.

But there is an increasing awareness in Germany of the need to show more understanding of the way others see them. The Federal German President, Richard Weizsäcker, has recently been outspoken on the subject of guilt. He says that he does not think that there is any such thing as the guilt of an entire nation but he deplores the attempt by too many people to avoid taking note of what has happened. Germany, he has proclaimed, 'must accept the past, Germany was responsible for the War'.

You may find it surprising that I should single out this remark – to you a statement of the obvious – but coming from a West German leader it was significant; it not only dealt with the question of guilt about the past, but, like an apparently unimportant move on the chess board, say of a pawn one square forward, it opened up new lines of action.

In the course of this lecture I shall be making sweeping generalizations because they give life and meaning to the interplay of nations; and I shall make a broad assertion here that West Germany is the only country in the Western world in which, over the past forty years or so, foreign policy has regularly dominated domestic policy.

In matters of policy, West German leaders have consistently shown sensitivity about the bearing of the past on present relations with the outside world. This has had a lot to do with the reluctance of the Federal Republic to stop being a political pygmy long after it has become an economic giant. Today, despite its great economic power, West Germany still does not seek to play an independent role in the world or even in Europe. That is some measure of the continuing impact of its past.

The division of Germany underlies Bonn's foreign policy and differentiates it from that of other countries. 'The German Question', the euphemism by which reunification is known in the Federal Republic, has been revitalized by the present German Government. From 1969 until a year or so ago the subject had simmered quietly on the back burner where Chancellor Willy Brandt had relegated it in accordance with his policy of *Ostpolitik*, which presupposed the continuation of the status quo in Europe. This revitalization is the consequence of growing self-confidence, of the casting-off of guilt and of the acceptance of responsibility for things past, as President Weizsäcker has described it. A former German Foreign Minister, Dr Gerhard Schröder, a man of the right, but not of the extreme right, has recently urged Germans to be confident in pursuing the aim of reunification through self-determination, adding that 'the shadows of our past must not be allowed to lay us open to blackmail'. To me it came as a surprise when a year or two ago Franz Josef Strauss, the Prime Minister of Bavaria, a man decidedly of the right, promoted a large Deutschmark credit for the German Democratic Republic, thus showing that, for the right, inter-German relations overrode any inhibition about dealing with a Communist regime. Lately Helmut Schmidt has written, 'The East and West Germans share a profound wish to be reunited. ... No one should have any illusions – the Germans will be as stubborn as the Poles, who got together again after having been divided for almost 130 years.'

Where, you may wonder, is this German attitude leading; and what are the reactions of other countries, of France, the United States and ourselves, not to mention the Soviet Union? I have just attended a multi-national conference at Ditchley where the theme was 'Divided Germany and the Future of Europe'. One of the opening speakers declared emphatically that the subject of unification was dead. Nevertheless the debate on this dead issue was so lively that it went on longer than any previous discussion on any subject at Ditchley.

My own impression is that reunification is not in the forefront of the minds of most West Germans as they go about their daily business, but that it is there not far below the surface, like the topic of some lost or discredited relation whom one hopes one day to gather back into the fold. The Germans have a feeling, subconscious rather than acknowledged, that they have been unfortunately treated by history. After all, other countries have been able to bring state and nation together within the confines of the same frontier and have achieved fulfilment and stability in doing so. Why should it still elude the Germans? It is more like this I think, a sense that lasting unity is their due, rather than any yearnings for the days of Barbarossa and the Hohenstaufens or of Bismarck and Prussian leadership, let alone of Hitler and his *Grossdeutschland* solution. At the Ditchley Conference I have just mentioned the German representatives were insistent that something could and should be done to respond to the patriotic feelings of all Germans – to their national sense – even if this, in foreseeable circumstances, could not amount to the reunification of the two states.

What of course renders judgement on this subject particularly hazardous is the decentralization and diversification that have been encouraged in West Germany since the Second World War. The different Länder (administrative districts) are not becoming any more similar. The derogatory way in which a Bavarian talks of anyone living north of the Danube as 'a ghastly Prussian' is only to be compared with the contempt with which a Berliner speaks of someone from Munich. We should not forget that Bismarck described a Bavarian as being halfway between an Austrian and a human being.

While I doubt that in their heart of hearts the Germans have renounced reunification, I do not believe in the foreseeable future they will seek to bring it about by anything but peaceful means. Nor do I consider that they will be tempted to go off on a *Sonderweg* involving the renunciation of the Western Alliance and democratic government, and to plump instead for reunification on the basis of a neutrality which would inevitably subject them to Soviet hegemony. Such a wayward course would be no solution to Germans anywhere. As Chancellor Helmut Kohl put it in a remarkable lecture in Oxford in May 1984, 'it would not help the people of Leipzig to be reunited in a Communist Germany if the majority of Germans thereby surrendered their freedom'.

In the Soviet attitude there has been an important change. For a long time they paid lip-service to the idea of German reunification, as did the East Germans. The concept of unity was incorporated in the East German constitution and was referred to in the 1955 Friendship Treaty between the German Democratic Republic and the Soviet Union. The two subsequent Friendship Treaties made no reference to reunification but dealt with means of bringing the two countries more closely together. With West Germany's admission to NATO in 1955, Moscow – and East Germany – must have abandoned the hope of bringing about a reunified Germany under a pro-Soviet or neutral regime. From then on the policy both of Moscow and of East Berlin has been to consolidate the division of Germany. The West Germans have hoped to bring about some change in attitudes in the Democratic Republic through a policy of intensive contacts – *Wandel durch Annäherung* – but both Soviet and East German leaders have been bent upon the consolidation of the German Democratic Republic as a separate state, which is what it was recognized to be by the Basic Treaty signed between the two Germanies in 1972. The Soviet veto in 1984 on the proposed visit to the Federal Republic by the East German leader Erich Honecker and the evidence we have that Mikhail Gorbachev again vetoed such a visit in 1986, show how sensitive the Soviets are to any sign of too great an intimacy between the two Germanies.

The unequivocal Soviet opposition to reunification governs Western policy. Western leaders have to declare in public their support for reunification on the basis of self-determination, not only because the United States, Britain and France are committed to this by the Bonn/Paris Conventions of 1955, but because to do otherwise would risk undermining the confidence of West Germans in the West and tempt them to lend an ear to Eastern blandishments. Britain, like the United States and France, cannot escape responsibility for Berlin and 'Germany as whole' as this flows from the conclusion of the Second World War. But it is the Soviet Government which disposes; and whether or not the West German Government's allies would really favour reunification must depend upon the conditions under which reunification might take place. Meanwhile the dilemma remains: whereas a divided Germany in the heart of Europe is a source of instability, the idea of a reunified Germany can also be disturbing, because of the large number of Germans, their capabilities and their geographical position. I do not know what the French today would think if such a proposal were real. But I do recall the words of the former French Prime Minister Georges Clemenceau; 'The Germans would be bearable', he said, 'if there were twenty million fewer of them.'

There is another field in which the West German attitude differs from that of other Western countries: the Alliance and European unity. NATO, of course, provides indispensable security for the Federal Republic against the threat from the East. So it does for the other countries of the Alliance, but the Germans feel particularly exposed. They opted for the West in the 1940s and 1950s when the Americans had nuclear superiority. Now the defence shield of NATO can be depended upon less absolutely. How often have I heard Helmut Schmidt say that it would take a Soviet tank less than an hour to reach his home in Hamburg. To the West Germans the deterrent, and in particular the American military guarantee, are matters of life and death, not of argument.

Detente, which is the other side of the coin to deterrence, also has a particular connotation for the Germans. It is not just a way of managing relations between East and West – it is the only method of avoiding either military annihilation or Finlandization. It is their overriding concern. But to the West Germans (and, I believe, to other West Europeans) there is a positive side to detente and to normal relations with Russia: the advantages of promoting long-standing cultural and commercial links. 'I cannot imagine any of us', Helmut Schmidt has said recently, 'not feeling at home with people like Dostoevski, Tolstoy, Lermontov, Pushkin, Turgenev, Gogol, and nowadays, Pasternak and Solzhenitsyn.' The directors of an industrial enterprise in the Federal Republic – Mannesmann, for instance – could well say the same about those in Russia with whom their firm have done business for a very long time.

I would place high in the catalogue of West German traits their pursuit of *Ostpolitik*. *Ostpolitik* is not the same as detente. It is an extra German dimension to it, arising from Germany's past, from the division of the country and from its long-standing connections with Eastern Europe and Russia. It is a policy pioneered in the early 1970s by Chancellor Brandt and Egon Bahr, State Secretary in the Chancellor's office. It means something more than dialogue with the East: it implies the establishment of a stable relationship there and, not least important, the creation of a *modus operandi* between Germany's dismembered limbs. *Ostpolitik* aims not simply at serving the peaceful purposes of detente, but also at advancing the cause of German unity. I have heard that there is talk now of the Social Democratic Party in Germany favouring a second *Ostpolitik*, so successful is the first considered to have been.

Bonn's attachment to the idea of a closely integrated Western Europe arises from the conviction that, living as they do a nationally diminished and divided life, West Germans must have a wider identity than that provided by existing frontiers – an allegiance that is essential to head off the internal dangers of strident nationalism or, at the other extreme, of neutralism and the abandonment of democracy. Western European integration is also seen as assisting the new relationship with France and as enabling West Germany to play a part on the world's stage without being too prominent an actor. Finally, Chancellor Kohl has explained that it is only in concert with their Western allies that Federal Germany can hope to solve its national problem peacefully, that is the problem of unification in freedom and security.

One further speciality characterizing West German policy is reconciliation with France. From 1945 this has been paramount and has been pursued with a dedication by both the West Germans and the French which has been the wonder and, dare I say, sometimes the envy of the third side of the European triangle, Great Britain. Painful though it may be to us to have to recognize it, the French and Germans are indispensable to each other whereas Britain is to neither; and, alas, there has been little in our economic performance or political attitude to the idea of Western Europe over the past decade to increase our value as a partner. Our Gross Domestic Product (GDP) is half that of the Federal Republic and 15 per cent less than that of France. This discrepancy can be calibrated on the scale of summit meetings. Schmidt, I recall, in the run-up to his meetings with President Giscard d'Estaing, was always talking about 'my friend Valéry'. Their meetings were both more frequent and more informal than those between German and British leaders.

France and the French attitude to the outside world and French foreign policy are also, despite all the changes in economic and security relationships, governed by the past. But it is a very different past from that of Germany. It is imbued with a sense of what France stands for, and its undying message for the world, combined with an acute and even painful awareness of not so distant ignominy.

It is impossible to live in France today or do international business with the French without being reminded frequently of the glory of France, of its civilizing mission for other countries. To President de Gaulle, of course, this certain idea of France and of France's glory was an impulse behind all thought and action. But de Gaulle in this respect reflected a widespread and enduring attitude of which I was very much aware, thirty years after the end of the Second World War. President Giscard expressed the idea by the word *rayonnement*, for which I could never find an adequate rendering in English, though I suppose 'radiance' is the closest literal translation. He often linked it with what he described as France's mondialism. I suppose the word *esprit* may come into it too – another word I find untranslatable.

President François Mitterrand has called up the same voices, extolling 'this indefinable genius which enables France to understand and express the needs of the human spirit'. Furthermore, aware of the limitations on France's role as a world military power, Mitterrand has made much of France's appeal to the Third World. 'We have today', he declared from the Elysée Palace, 'a great *rayonnement* in the Third World. . . . Our policy corresponds best to their aspirations.'

What struck me often in Paris was the preoccupation with the concept of France, the self-consciousness about France and what it stood for, which was never anything mean or small or insignificant to others, but indeed something from which everyone stood to benefit. In one quite short speech Giscard used the word 'France' over twenty times.

I do not want to suggest that we in Britain are less nationally minded, but I think that we speak about it less, perhaps because we take our role for granted, and we make no claim to a universal civilizing mission – an attitude that may be seen as a sign of our insularity. Our imperialist spirit in its heyday was different from that of France, and in any case it no longer exists, whereas France believes that its light still reaches into every corner of the globe. Germany, I may interject, does not see itself as having any universal mission, and never has done. Prussian leadership of the first centralized German state in the last century had not even absorbed the spirit of the Enlightenment and had no political message for non-Germans.

When I was first appointed Ambassador to Paris, the French Ambassador in Bonn, where I was also serving, told me that he wanted to brief me about his country. 'Every day you are in France', he said, 'do not forget two facts: firstly, that we had a Revolution, such as you have never had; secondly, that we were defeated in 1940, and you were not. You will find these facts relevant to all your dealings with the French.'

I was to find this advice both wise and helpful. It struck me that their

Revolution helped to explain many French attitudes – to the state, to their rulers, to land and property. But more pertinent to what I was doing was the French conviction that the Revolution had permeated the universe for ever with the ideals of liberty, equality and fraternity. If Louis XIV had dazzled the world with power and glory, the Revolution had inspired it with the principles of self-determination and individual freedom. I had noticed when I lived in Poland how convinced the French were that the moral support – and the political asylum – they had accorded in the previous century to the Poles rebelling against tsarist domination had earned them a permanent place in Polish hearts. It was true.

This global mission is not allowed to eclipse the hard-headed interests of the French state. The French look after these with exceptional skill and assiduity. But I think that anyone dealing with France must be aware of the special role – the defender of liberty and the apostle of civilization – in which the French see themselves as cast on the world's stage. It explains, for instance, their attitude to Eastern Europe and their stance on Central America or South Africa. It means that much Gallic logic often has to be deployed to reconcile the apparent inconsistencies between principle and national interest, for example their signature of the pipe-line agreement with the Soviet Union in 1981 soon after declaring that relations with Moscow could not be normal so long as the Soviet oppression in Afghanistan and Poland persisted.

The defeat and humiliation of 1940, following the failure of the policy of appeasement, explains much that is otherwise surprising to a foreign observer: the absence of the pacifism, for instance, that permeated French thought in the 1930s, and the emphasis on independence and military self-reliance. The independent nuclear force is necessary not only to guarantee the security of Western Europe from Soviet attack but to avoid dependence on the United States. Nineteen-forty also partly explains the extraordinary facts that both the French Socialist and the French Communist Parties support their country's independent nuclear force, and that there is no pressure from the left in France to shift resources from defence to welfare. The sinking of the Greenpeace ship *Rainbow Warrior* last year generated little internal criticism beyond the pages of *Le Monde*, despite the affront given to Third World opinion. This was judged less important than the need to provide for France's security. Chernobyl has produced in France much less agitation about the dangers of nuclear power than has been aroused elsewhere.

Just as France must seek to be independent militarily so it must be independent ideologically. Hence the frequent high-level visits between French and Soviet and East European leaders since the end of the Second World War; and hence the French view that detente must embrace ideological as well as military detente. The most traditional of all French policies has been the *alliance de revers*, friendship with the neighbours and potential rivals of one's potential enemy regardless of their systems of government; and I see ideological detente as a manifestation of this in modern guise.

Likewise owing something to 1940 are the views of French leaders about Britain. These are apt to oscillate between rivalry and contempt. When I first arrived in Paris, some ten years ago now, I was struck by the way I was received at the Quai d'Orsay. It was perfectly polite, if a little more formal than in London. I would be ushered by a *huissier* into that imposing palace, convey to the official of the Quai in as amicable a way as I could the pellet of an opinion that London had asked me to transmit and then receive my interlocutor's reply. But often, in my early days in Paris, I would then find that he would detain me and, as if reaching into the drawer of his desk for some Pandora's box of problems, he would go on to say that he wished to raise with me, on behalf of the French Government, some objection about some speech or activity or non-activity for which the British Government were responsible. The protest was rarely germane to the subject I had originally raised, and after this had happened several times I began to think that there must be a standing instruction obliging French officials to use any visit by a British representative to raise some objection drawn from a set list of complaints. I do not think that this was simply residual Gaullism. It seemed to me, at any rate in those days, that the French had a 'Trojan horse' fixation about us, fearing that we would insinuate unwanted American ideas or influence into the European camp. Not, I must emphasize, that the French have a deep-seated dislike of the American people. I think as a generalization that of the much-targeted Anglo-Saxons it is we rather than the Americans who are the victims of most of their barbs. The United States after all is too powerful to excite either envy or derision, and I have often noticed how impressed the French are by the technology and vast resources of the Americans.

I do not want to give a false impression about the French view of us; and on the whole I regard them as fairer about us, and certainly as less governed by insular prejudice, than we are towards them. I have been struck too by the way the climate can change, moving from stormy to fair, whether in consequence of shifting economic circumstances or personal whim. President Giscard, for instance, was, I believe, much affected by the state visit he paid to this country as a guest of the Queen. You may think I am exaggerating when I say that state visits – which to the public may chiefly conjure up exchanges of presents and platitudes, gala dinners and traffic jams and occasionally the award of an honorary degree – may have a bearing on the attitude of the leaders of one country to those of another. But since 1904, the *annus mirabilis* of state visits between France and Britain, there is no doubt that they at times have done so.

One last question concerning France's attitude to this country: why should the French, so insistent on independence, be so critical of Britain, as they consistently have been, for our reluctance to give up our sovereignty in favour of a West European union? The founders of France's belief in an integrated Western Europe were Jean Monnet and Robert Schuman. What these two men had principally in mind in those days of 1948–50 was the need to provide a framework for Franco-German reconciliation and co-operation; and they began by creating the Coal and Steel Community. Their creed then developed into a desire for closer European economic integration more generally, with some merger of sovereignty as the Holy Grail. Monnet, commenting on the British refusal to join the Common Market negotiations some thirty years ago, put his finger on one of the main differences in the way we look at things compared with our Continental neighbours. 'You British', he said, 'always find it difficult to accept principles and prefer to make your decisions on the basis of facts. We on the Continent first set out the principles, believing that the facts will emerge later. They will emerge in our Communities and, when they do, you British will join us.' And so we did – but too late to influence the shape of the Community.

In France and Germany I found frequent exasperation, not so much over our much vaunted reliance on pragmatism, as over our failure to understand why our Continental neighbours, who have experienced greater national instability than we have ever done, need some concept, some institutionalized framework within which public life can be conducted. This difference between our empirical approach to politics and international affairs, and the analytical and conceptual one of the Continent, lies at the root of many of our problems with our partners in Europe.

Not all those attached in France to the idea of European unity see it as involving any considerable surrender of sovereignty. Indeed, few of today's political leaders would want that. But, without there being much excitement about it, I believe that there would be a consensus in France for the view that closer integration of Western Europe would be worthwhile for France and for Europe and that such a union would be greater than the sum of its parts. It would be a way of holding Germany. It would enable France to play a greater role than the confines of the present state permit. Continental Europe to them is where they ruled the roost for centuries; it is an extension of themselves. It is where they belong – in a way that Britain does not. Above all such integration would enable Western Europe to create for itself a force and influence in the world that is distinct from that of the superpowers.

Allowing for the fact that sweeping assertions about the United States of America must be as 'broad and general as the casing air', I maintain that America's approach to foreign policy is still suffused with the belief that capitalism, epitomized by the Americans themselves, is not just materially advantageous but ethically desirable; that the spread of market forces throughout the world must be good for everyone (as well as for the Americans); and indeed that people worldwide would come to realize its superior benefits if only they had the freedom to see and hear about them. There is something reminiscent here of Britain's mid-Victorian liberalism, which was the leitmotiv of its foreign policy in the last century: that man's interests are not inherently in conflict, and that in conditions of peace, and with freedom of trade, countries will complement each other rather than rival each other. This is the contrary of the view that the world is a jungle with everything up for grabs and man essentially a selfish and Hobbesian being. The Americans, as a general rule, do not see the globe as populated by Hobbesian creatures; it is one of the reasons for two other distinguishing features of their outlook on the world – generosity and optimism. I know that some people will argue that much of America's largesse – the Marshall Plan, for instance – has been promoted by national interest. There is some truth in this, motivation in public life being often as mixed as in private life, but I do assert that the Americans are open-handed, just as they are sublimely confident that the world will become a better place.

From early days the United States has been driven by the alternating currents of idealism and self-interest. The Founding Fathers believed that their high-minded principles would be adopted by other countries. George Washington's rejection of permanent alliances was a policy of isolation from contaminating influences as well as from involvement in other people's quarrels. President Abraham Lincoln said, *en route* to his Inauguration, that the Declaration of Independence gave 'liberty not alone to the people of this country, but hope to the world for all future time'.

President Woodrow Wilson insisted that the United States 'was the only idealistic nation in the world'. It was he who sent American troops to Archangel and Vladivostok in an anti-Communist crusade. It is sometimes difficult to differentiate between American idealism and puritanism. Thus, although President Franklin Roosevelt was primarily a realist, there was an ideological or puritanical streak in him which came to the surface in his resistance to the post-war re-establishment of the European empires in Asia.

The Reagan Administration is second to none in its messianic zeal. 'I have always believed', President Ronald Reagan said two years after being elected President, 'that this anointed land was set apart in an uncommon way, that a divine plan placed this great continent here, to be found by people from every corner of the earth who had a special love of faith and freedom.' Professor Arthur Schlesinger has pointed out that this American belief in their own virtue is matched by an equally firm conviction in the wickedness of the Soviet Union. 'The Soviet Union underlies all the unrest that is going on' – these are President Reagan's words – 'if they weren't engaged in this game of dominoes there wouldn't be any hot spots in the world.' Despite the meeting with Gorbachev last year I suspect that President Reagan and his closest advisers still harbour this Manichaean view.

In a recent message to Congress, on 14 March 1986, Reagan has stressed the ideological stamp of his policy. In the 1970s, so the message runs, when the United States was weak 'the Soviets overreached' into Afghanistan, Angola, Cambodia, Ethiopia and Nicaragua. The United States, which has as its fundamental goal the advancing of 'the cause of democracy, freedom and human rights throughout the world', must therefore maintain its strength. This policy has been described as 'containment plus', or perhaps more descriptively as 'roll-back revisited'.

Although an underlying theme of US foreign policy has been a theoretical dislike of 'spheres of influence' as being somehow immoral, in practice the US Government have shown the greatest regard for the defence of their own backyard from the time of the Monroe Doctrine. The despatch of troops to the Dominican Republic in 1965 and more recently into Grenada, not to mention US policy in El Salvador and Nicaragua (to which the Reagan Administration gave first priority), are evidence of Washington's readiness to look after America's own geopolitical interests. I am not suggesting that there is anything wrong or exceptional in this. Other countries do the same. What is distinctive about America's behaviour is that it is cloaked in self-righteousness, reminiscent, again, of Britain in the nineteenth century.

In his book *The Nature of American Politics*, Professor Herbert Nicholas has drawn a parallel between the way Americans both revere and flout their domestic law and their similar ambivalence towards international engagements. They pay lip-service to the letter and spirit of treaties but show an insouciant disregard for such commitments whenever national interests are threatened, as over Grenada. I would only add that what was right about Grenada was that it succeeded. What was wrong about Kennedy's Bay of Pigs landing in Cuba was that it failed. Had Grenada gone wrong there would have been imprecations about the neglect of moral principles. I may interject that, impressed by the legalism prevalent in the United States, Maynard Keynes surmised that the *Mayflower* must have been full of lawyers, albeit puritan lawyers.

The alternation in Washington between idealism and self-interest was manifested to me by the roller-coaster trajectory through which President Jimmy Carter careered. Coming to the White House on the crest of a moral wave – the 'high road', my predecessor in the British Embassy in Washington called it – he was confronted by the hard realities of Soviet and Iranian policy: the Soviet invasion of Afghanistan and the Khomeini revolution. He imposed a grain embargo on the Soviet Union, and he guaranteed the integrity of the Persian Gulf against outside attack, which amounted to a very considerable extension of America's military commitment.

When the Republicans came to power in 1981, Secretary of State Alexander Haig declared that the United States would never acquiesce in the Soviet occupation of Afghanistan; but at the same time President Reagan announced that the grain embargo imposed by Carter after the invasion of Afghanistan would be lifted. One of my most unforgettable memories of Washington is of Mrs Thatcher in the White House giving a piece of her mind on this subject to President Reagan, Vice-President George Bush and the President's chief advisers, who were seated on a sofa in a row opposite her. She was explaining very patiently why the American policy of trying to prevent the Europeans from participating in the Siberian gas pipe-line was untenable. Surely they must see how wrong, how inconsistent, they were, having lifted their own grain embargo. Her American audience listened; they were chastened; and eventually US policy changed – without any explanation, let alone recrimination. That is the American way.

One conspicuous feature of the US approach to foreign policy is their belief that all problems can and should be solved, rather than just managed: that comprehensive and final results can be achieved between countries, just as they are between individuals, provided enough intelligence and resources are devoted to the problem. Of course this does sometimes mean the injection of much-needed fuel into the otherwise sluggish engine of diplomacy; and, to be sure, far-reaching solutions were achieved soon after the Second World War with the Marshall Plan and NATO. But the United States was then all-powerful economically and militarily and it was a question of their readiness to make resources available unilaterally to Western Europe. But when in the early 1970s Dr Henry Kissinger, then National Security Adviser, proposed the 'Year of Europe' seeking a new all-embracing relationship between the two sides of the Atlantic, no solution was forthcoming. Indeed, the result was a deterioration in relations between the United States and Europe, because the European countries did not think that every problem could be wrapped up in what the Americans called at the time 'one ball of wax'. Part of the trouble for Britain arose from Kissinger's conceptual approach to the conduct of foreign policy – his search for a grand design – the sort of idea that is apt to make the British wince.

I have to interject here that America's readiness to learn from its mistakes, for example, over Vietnam, has been remarkable. It is not something that other countries, say France or Germany, have in the past found easy. This adaptability is partly caused by the diffuse nature of the US decision-making process and the power of the lobbyists.

In the early days of the Reagan Administration, when there was much rhetoric about the evil Soviet empire, I paid a call on a senior adviser in the White House. We discussed how to deal with the Soviet Union. I questioned whether sanctions, such as those the US Government then favoured, would really have much impact on the Soviet Union. The adviser handed me a piece of paper, saying that the opinion he received was the opposite of this. He assured me that I would see from this single sheet of analysis, prepared by a high intelligence authority, that there were good grounds for believing that the whole Soviet system could be overthrown provided a little pressure was exerted. Looking back I realize that my reaction was tiresome. How I wish I had been able to show incredulity without that sniff of old world superiority to which Americans are so sensitive.

The US tendency to look for panaceas in international affairs is linked with their confidence in the beneficial effects of technology. The great success of the Manhattan Project in producing the atomic bomb may have had something to do with this. More recently the enthusiasm for Star Wars is a further reflection of this confidence. It seems to me at times as though the body of American policy is being wagged by the tail of technology: for instance, very little attempt is made to analyse Soviet intentions, beyond the sweeping assumption that they are aggressive, compared with the intense brain-power devoted to weaponry.

It is, of course, impossible to live in the United States without being impressed by their technological and economic might. But one also has to realize that this might does encourage Americans to think that they can do everything on their own militarily; in this sense there is a tendency to overlook the need for allies, except to provide political backing for policies the Americans have already decided upon. They certainly do not like being on their own politically. In his message of 14 March 1986, from which I have already quoted, Reagan spoke of America's 'understandable reluctance to shoulder alone burdens that are properly shared with others'. This phrase contained a coded message – but it is an easily breakable code – signalling America's growing impatience with its European allies. We are apt to complain to the Americans about their failure to consult their allies before taking action. I do not myself think that such failures are usually caused by forgetfulness on America's part. There are times when they believe that by some quick move they can achieve the desired result by themselves; and we must not forget for how long in their history isolationism was the dominant theme. The American failure to consult the Europeans before rejecting the compromise formula for an Intermediate-range Nuclear Force (INF) limitation agreement in 1982, or President Reagan's declaration the following year that Star Wars were going to 'change the course of history', without any consultation with allies, or the President's decision to invade Grenada with debonair indifference to the susceptibilities of London – these sins of omission on Washington's part were deliberate: they did not want to be delayed or frustrated by discussion with hesitant allies. We must bear in mind that when

Mrs Thatcher was involved with service chiefs and other Ministers in hectic discussions after the Argentine invasion of the Falklands she did not, so far as I know, consult the US Government before deciding to send the British Fleet to the South Atlantic – although this decision significantly affected US interests and could not have been carried to a successful conclusion without American support.

The air strike by the USA against Libya in April 1986 in reprisal for Libya's involvement in international terrorism is the most recent and typical example of the American belief in quick solutions. I myself have a vivid recollection of the hostage rescue operation in Iran in 1981. There were a number of things about this operation which were extraordinary to the outside observer – and I am not referring to one's surprise that, with all their military intelligence and experience, the US Administration should ever have thought it could work. What was astonishing was that the new patriotism which the hostage drama seemed to engender in the United States was devoid of any sense that imperial pride had been offended – as it had been, for instance, in Britain at the time of the murder of General Gordon in the last century. However, as has frequently been brought home to me, the Americans do not nourish any imperial feeling. Certainly they must safeguard their own hemisphere and try to arrest the spread of Communism but they do not wish to order other people about. They do not display pomp or panoply. They are not by nature the world's policemen. What was wrong with President Carter in the eyes of his compatriots was not his lack of a sufficiently forward policy but the impression he gave of irresolution, his lack of dignity, his reliance on prayer and pious hope. The former Israeli Foreign Minister, Abba Eban, has pertinently applied to the Carter Administration the words Tacitus used of a Roman emperor; *capax imperii nisi imperasset*.[1] Of course President John F. Kennedy in his inaugural address delivered what amounted to a doctrine of universal commitment on behalf of all those anywhere in the world who felt threatened. But he was not seeking to extend American dominion, any more than President Harry S. Truman had been doing in the doctrine which he declared on 12 March 1947, nor Reagan in his statement on foreign policy on 14 March 1986.

I have mentioned the traditional isolationism of the United States which to this day lurks not far below the surface of many American minds. But even those who may sigh nostalgically for a return to the good old days cannot overlook a dramatic recent change that has come over American economic life. Ten years ago, foreign trade – exports and imports – amounted to only

---

[1] *Maior privato visus dum privatus fuit, et omnium consensu capax imperii nisi imperasset*: 'When he was a commoner he seemed too big for his station, and had he never been emperor, no one would have doubted his ability to reign'.

8 per cent of US GDP; the figure is now over 20 per cent. This greater commercial dependence obviously has an important impact on Washington's attitude to the outside world.

Another American tendency of which one has to be aware in trying to gauge the likely US reaction on any foreign policy issue is what can be described as 'either/or-ism'. 'Our ways of thinking', Secretary of State George Shultz has written, 'have tended too often to focus either on increasing our strength or on pursuing negotiation.' He meant of course that Americans do not readily see that these must go hand in hand. The initial decision of the incoming Reagan Administration to suspend nuclear arms negotiations with the Russians until the United States had once again improved the balance in its favour is an example both of this tendency and, I suggest, of a capacity to misread Soviet psychology.

Finally, one might ask how the United States looks on Western Europe and, more particularly, on Britain at the present time. To what extent do we still count? Certainly there is some talk nowadays among Americans about the Far East having supplanted Western Europe as the area most important to the United States. It is true that industrially and technologically Europe has been overtaken by Japan and the countries of the Pacific Basin, and that over half of America's trade is now with the Far East. Relevant, too, is the evident attenuation of the Soviet threat to Western Europe, which for two decades after the Second World War engaged US attention so acutely. A quarter of the US population is now of non-European origin, a shift that is also pertinent to this argument. But I believe that despite these changes Europe remains the focus of America's interest, not simply because half US direct investments abroad are in Europe, but because any fundamental change in the status quo in Western Europe would be regarded as having a direct impact on Washington's strategic–political interests.

As for Britain, it is surprising that, despite all the changes in both countries and the discrepancy between us in power, we do still matter to the Americans; their relationship with us is different from that with other countries. I do not mean, of course, that we always see eye to eye or that there are not strong anti-British groups in the United States; or that other countries do not have particular relationships with the United States or great influence there. Since the Second World War I believe that our relationship has turned a good deal on defence: if we were no longer a nuclear power it would count for less. In the whole period of forty years since the end of the Second World War I suppose the worst moment in Anglo-American history was Suez. My impression is that the Americans in retrospect are no prouder of their role at that time than we should be of ours. I was struck during the Falklands crisis by the number of times Haig said to me that whatever occurred they were not going to repeat what happened over Suez.

You may have read the assertion made in Washington after the Libyan raid that one of the reasons for using F1-11s based in Britain was to bring about British involvement and therefore to avoid giving the impression that the operation was purely an American one. This was thought desirable from the point of view of world public opinion – the need for political allies that I have mentioned. I do not know the truth of this; but it may have counted in some minds in Washington. My experience of decisions in that town is that the process is so diffuse that there is rarely one single impulse, or one single source. But at any rate the idea gives some indication of our continuing relevance to the United States, Of course, it also makes life more difficult for Mrs Thatcher, who, as a result of the Libyan raid, has been accused of being President Reagan's poodle. Indeed, I hear that there is a particular exercise now going on in Whitehall in order to counteract this sentiment – it is known as depoodlerization.

At one meeting in Washington with the Ambassadors of the other European countries, I moaned that the British did not have a lobby in Washington such as the Italians had or the Israelis. My European colleagues threw up their hands in astonishment, protesting that the whole place was our lobby. This must be taken with a large pinch of salt. What I do believe, however, is that the very fact that the ethnological make-up of the United States has changed so enormously in recent times has, paradoxically, increased the relevance of the original connection. If the United States is to retain some sort of national identity and cohesion, it must accentuate what lies at its roots, and what is fundamental to it – its language, and the values and traditions upon which it is founded.

I do not, in conclusion, wish to make too much of historic parallels as a guide to action, because they have led to some disastrous decisions in modern times. But I am convinced that awareness of how other countries see the outside world and how they believe their national needs can be met is essential to understanding or conducting international relations. Diplomacy is after all the art of getting your way by putting yourself in other people's shoes.

AMERICA AND THE FALKLANDS

First published in The Economist,
12 November 1983

Since the time of President Monroe we have known how sensitive the American Government is to any European involvement in the American hemisphere. But events recently reveal a surprising extension of his doctrine. The Americans seem to look upon the Europeans as under some sort of obligation to sympathize, and even to support them, in their policies towards Latin America and the Caribbean. The rationale now is anti-Communism, whereas Monroe's original impulse was of course anti-colonialism. A new sensitivity is also developing the other way round: the Europeans are ready to criticize the Americans for what they do in their own backyard, but they expect American support when their interests are threatened across the Atlantic.

Over the Grenada crisis, the British tend to say that the Americans acted impetuously in using force instead of trying to solve the problem by other means first, a method which Washington had insisted that London pursue after the Argentine attack on the Falkland islands. Today the Americans are bitter that the British have let them down by not supporting them, at least morally, in their action in the Caribbean, a dereliction that is deplorable in view of the American Government's stalwart support for London over the Falklands. After this bruising, and the election in November 1983 in Argentina of a civilian president, it may be a good moment for one participant to look back at the Falklands episode.

From Invasion to American Tilt

The intensity of United States diplomacy over the Falklands can only be understood if it is realized how closely the American public followed what was going on. From the Argentine invasion to the surrender of Port Stanley, the Falklands crisis was front-page news and the lead story for television in America every day.

At the outset of the crisis in April 1982, many Americans saw it in Gilbert and Sullivan terms. President Reagan described the place as 'that little ice-cold bunch of land down there'. When it became clear that Britain was in earnest, doubts began to be expressed by military experts, on television and in the press, about our capability to mount a successful military operation in the South Atlantic. There were fears that the United States might become embroiled – mutterings of another Vietnam. The sinking of the *Sheffield* produced almost as dreadful an impact in America as in Britain.

When we came to re-establish forces on the islands the Americans began to worry, not that we would get into a military impasse, but that we would succeed so overwhelmingly as to humiliate the Argentines. As the prospect of a bloody battle loomed, American public opinion began to worry more. It is fair to generalize that throughout the crisis, and whatever the military prognosis, the Americans always hoped that there would be a diplomatic rather than a military outcome.

By nature combative, the Secretary of State Alexander Haig nevertheless embodied the national will in his search for peace rather than battle in the South Atlantic. He never wavered in two convictions: that the Argentines had been guilty of aggression and must not be allowed to get away with it or there would be dire consequences for the rest of the world, not least the American hemisphere; and that no good would redound to either side in the long run from a military solution, which would also cause great difficulties for the United States.

He believed that, if he was to have any chance of success in his negotiation, the American Government must avoid taking sides; instead it should give the impression of complete impartiality. The neutral posture maintained by America until the end of April was difficult for people to understand on the other side of the Atlantic, where it was thought that the United States should not fail to stick by an ally, particularly when it had been a victim of blatant aggression.

The Americans were always worried about an increase of Soviet influence in Argentina and throughout Latin America. They were concerned too that any overt tilt towards Britain would jeopardize American interests in Latin America; and it is true that once they did plump for us they became as much the target for Latin American obloquy as we were.

Haig emphasized to me in the early days that the United States was not at heart impartial, that the British Government had always supported the Reagan Administration in foreign policy, and that America could not privately be even-handed in anything involving its closest ally. Publicly, however, its spokesmen said that the United States intended to steer a course 'down the middle' and not to give any help either way. 'It's a very difficult situation for the United States,' President Reagan pleaded in answer to a press question on 6 April, 'because we're friends with both of the countries engaged in this dispute ...' The President had to listen to those who struck a cautious note about the dangers for America in becoming too involved too soon on the British side and about the absolute need for the United States to be seen to be promoting peace. I have been told subsequently by those closest to the President how hard it was for him to distance himself from the Latin Americans. But Haig frequently assured me at the time that, notwithstanding the public stance, the President was our staunch supporter.

Haig went out of his way several times in the following weeks to promise me that there would be no repeat of Suez. Given the possible parallels. I do not think his assurances were otiose. The Falklands crisis touched on certain American nerves that had proved sensitive at Suez: a recessive feeling about colonialism; concern that the British were expecting the United States eventually to pick up the cheque; worry about the Russians; and the fear that what Britain was doing would rally other countries in the area against Western interests.

Much has been written about the influence of the 'latino lobby' on the American Government's policy over the Falklands crisis. Ambassador Thomas Enders, the imposing Under-Secretary in the State Department dealing with Latin America, had visited Buenos Aires in March when he had derived no inkling of any Argentine intention to move to military confrontation with us. On 31 March he told Haig, in my presence, that the US Government had had an assurance from the Argentine Foreign Minister that the Argentines were not contemplating any military action, a promise that had just been confirmed. Enders always kept American requirements in Latin America in the forefront of his mind, as it was his business to do.

Jeane Kirkpatrick, America's Ambassador to the United Nations, who held both Cabinet rank and the President's ear, had her own special arguments for believing that the United States should not make a choice between Britain and Argentina. She did not consider that Argentina could fairly be accused of aggression given the fact that it was simply asserting a long-stated claim to the islands. It was she who had been the most prominent apostle of the creed that a sharp distinction must be drawn between authoritarian and totalitarian regimes; Argentina being a prime example of the former, this justified a positive diplomatic attitude on the part of the United States. Besides, the Government in Buenos Aires had been giving America support for its covert operations in Central America and its anti-Communist causes throughout Latin America, a stance, let it be admitted, that might well, in the eyes of the Argentine junta, have secured American acquiescence in a forward Argentine policy over the Falklands.

In the United States Congress the influence of the 'latino lobby' proved to be slight. Even those who were ready to criticize London over Northern Ireland – for example Senators Kennedy and Moynihan and Speaker O'Neill – came to back us publicly on the Falklands. In the course of visits I paid to members of the Senate Foreign Relations Committee, one Senator expostulated to me, after I had held forth at some length on the importance of upholding in practice the principle of self-determination, particularly in the American hemisphere: 'Forget it, Mr Ambassador, do you think that if it had been Brazil that had been in the Falklands and if Argentina had invaded we would have felt so strongly? It is because you are British.' My inclination to see in this an important message for British–American relations generally was tempered by evidence that those who by reflex were sympathetic to us and unsympathetic to a military dictatorship tended sometimes to harbour inhibitions about continued colonial rule in the Falklands.

However, congressional opinion was generally helpful to us and we should be grateful: the Senate passed a resolution in our favour at the end of April, and the House of Representatives did the same shortly afterwards.

Haig Becomes Involved

On becoming Foreign Secretary immediately after Argentina's invasion, Francis Pym sent Haig a message: Her Majesty's Government was determined to secure the withdrawal of Argentine forces and the restoration of British administration by whatever means were necessary; the role of the United States would be critical. When I conveyed this to Haig on the same day, 6 April, he said that he was thinking of some sort of mediation; he surmised that it might be possible to think of negotiating with us and the Argentines some mixed administration to run the islands.

I said that I must clarify the British Government's attitude to avoid any risk of misunderstanding. Our Government could not enter into any negotiations about the future of the Falkland islands until Argentine troops had been withdrawn. The same would be true of the US Administration *mutatis mutandis* if American territory were occupied. If, for example, the Cubans, with Soviet support, occupied Puerto Rico, the Americans would not be ready to enter into a negotiation on the future of the island while Cuban troops were still in occupation.

It seemed to me, so I told Haig, inopportune to think in terms of some multilateral administration of the islands. We were prepared to talk about the future of the islands and their relations with Argentina only when Argentine troops had withdrawn and our administration had been restored.

Haig said that he could not see how General Galtieri could survive if he simply had to take away Argentine troops without getting anything in return. I said that it was not our purpose to help Galtieri survive. It was he who had brought about the present occupation in order to distract public opinion from economic and political difficulties.

I asked Haig to understand the strength of British opinion. There could scarcely have been an issue since 1939 upon which the British felt so strongly, and this feeling ran across party lines. No government in Britain could possibly contemplate a negotiation involving the Argentines while they remained in occupation of the islands. If the question was asked why we bothered so much about 2,000 people at the other end of the world, a point that had been made to me in many public interviews, the answer was that the Americans should bear in mind how strongly they had felt about fifty-two hostages in Iran: what was at issue here was whether, in the American hemisphere, differences were going to be settled by force, and whether the principle of self-determination, which the United States had pioneered, was going to be overthrown. Haig, therefore, should be in no doubt of our determination and our ability to go through with this operation.

The Secretary of State said that he entirely understood. He was completely aware of the state of British public opinion on this issue. He was determined, as was the President, to do everything conceivable to help the British Government. I should not underestimate the personal involvement of the President in this matter. He was very conscious of the problems and views of the Prime Minister. But the difficulty, Haig went on, was how to get the Argentines out. He accepted it now as a fact that they must be got out before the British could enter a negotiation. But, thinking aloud, he wondered whether it would be possible for him to appoint a commission comprising, say, some distinguished but impartial American figure, a Canadian, some Latin Americans and one or two others, who might act as intermediaries and serve as some kind of interim administration.

Haig then offered ideas about involving the Organization of American States (OAS). I said that this would be totally deplorable. The Americans, scarcely less than ourselves, were regarded as Anglo-Saxon gringos by that organization and we would get nowhere by involving them. Nor, I said, would there be any point in bringing in the United Nations again. We had got a very satisfactory 10-1 vote in the UN Security Council (Resolution 502) on 3 April, and it was important to base ourselves on this resounding demand for Argentine withdrawal.

When discussing the American attitude towards the Argentines, Haig said, with strong support from Enders, who was present at the meeting, how important it was for the Americans not to lean too openly towards the British side because, if they did, this would lose them credibility with the Argentines. Haig believed that the Americans alone could exert influence in Buenos Aires.

I said that President Reagan had not been able to avert the Argentine invasion; by the time he had got in touch with Galtieri, only shortly before the landings, it was too late to stop them. This did not mean that the Argentines would not be susceptible to American pressure. The Argentine regime was in dire economic straits and vulnerable to all manner of influence that the Americans could bring to bear on them. I presumed that the Americans would not be letting any further arms deliveries go to Argentina, and Haig confirmed categorically that this was so.

In reporting this initial talk with Haig following the Argentine invasion, I emphasized to London that he was not claiming to be putting forward any clearcut plan of action. He was simply trying to test initial reactions.

In the course of Haig's two visits to both London and Buenos Aires and visits by Pym and the Argentine Foreign Minister to Washington, Haig was trying to bridge a gap that may be described, at the risk of over-simplification, as follows:

> The Argentines were not prepared to accept any settlement that did not provide either for negotiations on sovereignty, to be concluded in their favour within a specific time-limit, or for an interim regime for the islands, after the withdrawal of forces by both sides, that would promote the acquisition of sovereignty by administrative means, including population and economic transfers. The British Government insisted that Argentine troops must withdraw, that sovereignty was theirs, that the traditional administration of the islands must be restored and that there must be no infringement of the right of the islanders to decide their own future.

Mrs Thatcher left Haig in no doubt at the very first meetings that she wanted a diplomatic solution but that force would be used if necessary. There was national determination not to appease a dictator. We could not negotiate under duress. Equally categorical, from the start, was Haig's insistence that some device was needed to bring about Argentine withdrawal without total loss of face. He spoke of the mentality of the Argentines, of the dangers of increased Soviet influence, of the great hazards to the British of a military landing and of the possibility that American opinion might become less favourable to Britain in the absence of a negotiated solution. The clue, in his judgement, was to be found in the avoidance by Britain of any unequivocal assertion of sovereignty and in the creation of some international umbrella. The Prime Minister questioned the purpose of this umbrella, to which Haig replied that he was deliberately seeking an arrangement which had 'certain constructive ambiguities'.

I think that this first round in London made a strong impact on Haig. He had been left in absolutely no doubt that London required the Argentines to withdraw as the first essential step. Mrs Thatcher was prepared to negotiate but not to yield to force, and she was 'very tough', to use Haig's words to me, to which he added, 'I wish we had more like her.'

I think there is a tendency, now that it is all over so successfully, to look back and see the military solution as the obvious one and to wonder what all the palaver over peace plans was about. But, if an account is to be given of how things really were at the time, it must not be forgotten that when the British task force was despatched to the South Atlantic few of those responsible for the decision had any idea how the Argentines were going to be ejected by force from the islands. According to my information, nobody involved in that decision thought at the time that it would be bound to lead to open war. Admiral Sandy Woodward has said, referring to the length of time that it took to get the task force to the South Atlantic, that this was 'an invaluable period of military preparation, and time for the politicos to try to resolve the issue without resorting to force'. So the admiral in charge of the task force was allowing at the start for a diplomatic solution, even though he could not depend upon it.[1]

'I hope that people realize', Admiral John Fieldhouse, Chief of Naval Staff and First Sea Lord, said on a visit to Ascension Island in April, 'that this is the most difficult thing that we have attempted since the Second World War.' At this stage, in the third week of April, I do not believe that the Royal Navy really believed it would be war. As for the British public, it was probably in favour of the despatch of the task force but was not at all glorying in the prospect of battle, a distinction the junta probably did not understand, while drawing confidently the wrong conclusion that it meant we would ultimately yield.

The strength of desire for negotiation swung in Whitehall with the tide of war. A great deal was at stake, the risks were very great and I know how much Ministers realized this. We had several bad moments, as at the start of our operation to retake South Georgia, or with the sinking of *Sheffield*. It was impossible to know what our casualties were likely to be, or how much British public opinion would tolerate in the way of losses. At the outset, too, Ministers had no reason to assume that the junta would prove totally irrational and a negotiated settlement did not seem unfeasible. I do not believe that anybody in the Government ever preferred the military route. A negotiated settlement was always the one most favoured, provided British interests and principles could be safeguarded. It was in the definition of these provisos and how they might be met that differences occurred within the British camp and between Washington and London. Conflict concentrated around what was essential for Britain's diplomatic needs and, inherent in this, how best to retain the sympathy and ultimately the practical support of the United States.

The time-factor was also crucial. The British task force could not hang about – or roll about – in the South Atlantic indefinitely while the Argentines dragged out negotiations, as they proceeded to do. Those who argue that Argentina's invasion might have been forestalled if an ultimatum had been given in advance have to overcome the fact that, even after we had despatched the task force, the Argentines, as Haig told me following long talks with them, did not believe that we were ready to fight.

Given its miscalculation about the likely British reaction, it is not surprising that Argentina should have been so intransigent diplomatically. After prolonged discussion with Haig who, on his return to Buenos Aires on 15 April, had been met by a vast demonstration organized by the junta to show the

---

[1] Admiral Sandy Woodward and General Jeremy Moore, *Journal of the Royal United Services Institute for Defence Studies*, March 1983.

public support for them over their Falklands policy, the Argentines put forward a proposal which Haig said, in transmitting it to Pym, was not something that he could urge the British Government to accept.

Their idea for troop withdrawals would heavily favour Argentina. At the end of the process, for instance, the British Fleet would have had to return to British ports, whereas the Argentines would be only a few hundred miles away. British administration would be re-established to a far lesser degree than under Haig's scheme and there would be a disproportionate representation of Argentines on the executive and legislative councils. The proposals opened up the possibility of an influx of Argentines into the islands. Finally, the text would exclude a return to the status quo ante and did not preserve the principle that the islanders should choose their own future.

The Argentines may well have been spinning out negotiations to gain time in the belief that: (1) the longer the *de facto* occupation, the readier would international opinion become to accept a *fait accompli*; and (2) with the advance of winter, the problems attendant upon an 8,000-mile supply line, and the threats posed by Argentine submarines and air forces, the British would increasingly doubt the feasibility of a landing and prolonged military presence in the South Atlantic.

But, as I have suggested, it would be wrong to give the impression that the Argentines were guided by some coherent and consistent strategy; or that it was ever clear to Haig what they were up to.

In a talk I had with Haig in Washington on 21 April, he described the irrationality and chaotic nature of the Argentine leadership. He said there seemed to be fifty people involved in decision-taking. If he reached some sort of agreement on one of the points at issue with a member of the junta, this was invariably countermanded by a corps commander entering the room an hour or so later. I asked Haig whether he thought that there was any point in continuing to negotiate with the present Argentine leaders. Were they not committed to a military solution and a military success? Haig said that he certainly had doubts on the subject. But he thought the Argentines were far from confident.

Pym arrived in Washington on 22 April for further talks. The Argentine Foreign Minister Costa Mendez arrived there on 25 April but refused to meet Haig because Britain had just retaken South Georgia. He spent his time drumming up support for the Argentine case at a forthcoming meeting of the Organization of American States. Messages whizzed between the three capitals. The upshot was a Haig plan put to both Governments on 27 April requiring a rapid yes or no answer. After the junta had referred the plan to corps commanders they replied in a manner that was construed by Haig as a rejection.

On 30 April, Haig made a statement that, while the United States had reasons to hope that Britain would consider a settlement on the lines of the American proposals of 27 April, Argentina had been unable to accept them. He announced that, in the light of Argentina's failure to accept a compromise, the American Government must take concrete steps to underscore that the United States cannot and will not condone the use of unlawful force to resolve disputes. He listed various restrictions on trade with Argentina, including military exports, and then declared that the President had directed that the United States would respond positively to requests for material support for British forces. There would, he said, of course, be no direct American military involvement.

In a message to Pym, Haig said:

> We will of course continue to support you in the OAS and in the UN and will be prepared to veto in the Security Council or vote against the General Assembly any resolutions which in our judgement depart from Security Council Resolution 502.

This was an important assurance.

The *Belgrano* and Peru

The American decision of 30 April to support Britain was a turning point in our fortunes. But it did not put an end to negotiations or to America's part in them. On the contrary, the American Government's desire to bring off a peaceful settlement grew with the likelihood of bloodshed in the South Atlantic.

I draw here on my own experience of the negotiations to deal with the assertion which continues to be made that negotiations with the Argentines might well have succeeded, and indeed were on the point of succeeding, when the Argentine cruiser *General Belgrano* was sunk. It is frequently alleged that the attack on the *Belgrano* was deliberately authorized by the Prime Minister to scupper negotiations, in the belief that a short, decisive military solution would be better for British interests than lengthy discussions leading to a negotiated settlement.

There have been several debates on the *Belgrano* sinking in the British Parliament. The new leader of the Labour Party has said that diplomatic negotiations looked promising at the time of the sinking; and he has demanded more information. The Argentine Foreign Minister at the time, Costa Mendez, has expressed the view, in an article published in *The Times* on 18 October 1983, that with the sinking of the *Belgrano* the possibility of a negotiated agreement was killed. Most of those who have written about the Falklands crisis, including the Insight team and Hastings and Jenkins, have been critical of the *Belgrano* sinking.[2] Most vociferous of all has been Tam Dalyell MP, who has recently been in Lima and is reported as saying, on the basis of evidence acquired there, that the sinking of the *Belgrano* was ordered by Mrs Thatcher to prevent the Peruvian peace plan succeeding. Dalyell has said twice incidentally in the British House of Commons that I went white when I heard the news of the sinking in Washington. So I have a personal reason to clear the record, if not my complexion.

On the afternoon of Saturday, 1 May, Pym arrived in Washington for the second weekend running. There was static in the air and the press everywhere. Some decisive development, whether diplomatic or military, was widely expected. Pym said publicly that the previous week he had come to Washington to visit a negotiator, this week to visit an ally, a remark that made some members of the American Administration wince. To me in private Pym spoke about the very tough mood at home reflected in the debate that had just taken place in the House of Commons.

He was acutely aware that the lines between military and diplomatic action, hitherto wide apart, were beginning to converge and would soon cross, compounding the high pitch of drama that each had reached. Port Stanley had been bombed by Vulcans that day; other attacks had been made on the islands by Harriers, of which one had been lost.

On Sunday, 2 May, at 19.00 hours GMT, 20.00 hours London time and 15.00 hours Washington time, the Argentine cruiser *Belgrano* was hit by the submarine *Conqueror* following a decision reached by the War Cabinet meeting at Chequers around midday.

It is not true, despite frequent allegations to that effect, that the Argentines had had no warning of our readiness to take military action outside the Maritime Exclusion Zone. On 23 April the British Government had announced its preparedness to attack any Argentine ship or aircraft wherever it was if it posed a threat to British forces in the South Atlantic. This was a highly important warning. It was conveyed immediately to the Argentine Government, circulated to the Security Council and released publicly. From that time any Argentine warship, submarine or military aircraft (including air transports used for reconnaissance) could expect to be attacked on or over the high seas. The Argentines have said subsequently that they were taken unawares by the attack. One can only say that this is not surprising given the endemic unawareness of the junta and their confidence that the British would never react militarily to the invasion of the islands.

During the morning (Washington time) of 2 May – though not over breakfast as has been suggested – Haig met Pym for a tête-à-tête that lasted

---

[2] The Sunday Times Insight Team, *The Falklands War* (André Deutsch, 1982), and Max Hastings and Simon Jenkins, *The Battle of the Falklands* (Michael Joseph, 1983).

two hours. He relayed President Reagan's conviction that British forces were 'doing the work of the free world', but then balanced this with an ardent plea that we could and should avoid a large-scale battle because it would be unnecessary and risky. He briefly outlined certain ideas which had originated in a Peruvian initiative and which had not been formulated in any definitive way. These were very similar to those he himself had advanced earlier and he thought they would be more acceptable in Buenos Aires if they were put forward by a South American Government. They could not possibly be described as 'proposals'.

Peru's seven-point plan (as the ideas later came to be called) was as follows:

(1) immediate ceasefire;
(2) mutual withdrawal of forces;
(3) involvement of third parties on a temporary basis in the administration of the islands;
(4) acceptance by both parties of the fact that a dispute over sovereignty exists;
(5) acknowledgement that the views and interests of the islanders must be taken into account in reaching a definitive settlement;
(6) formation of a contact group comprising Brazil, Peru, West Germany and the United States;
(7) the conclusion by 30 April 1983 of a definitive settlement for the working out of which the contact group would be responsible.

In his reply – as he has since confirmed publicly – Pym made it clear that, while he was very ready to consider any new ideas, what Haig had outlined was in essence not very different from his own scheme which had just been totally rejected by Argentina. Pym therefore wondered whether, if and when the details had been worked out, the Argentines were likely to take a different view. He emphasized that he would of course need to discuss any new ideas with his colleagues in London on his return. Haig fully agreed that more time and more detailed work were needed.

Pym and Haig saw each other again over lunch at the Embassy, and spoke again on the telephone before Pym flew to New York in the afternoon. It was only at this point that it was possible to telegraph a report to London: that telegram was despatched at 17.15 Washington time, or 22.15 London time.

Several critics have asked why, before giving their authority for the *Conqueror* to attack the *Belgrano*, British Ministers did not get in touch with Pym in Washington to make sure that nothing was going on there that might affect their decision. Tam Dalyell has described London's failure to check with Pym as 'mind-boggling'. The first comment to make is, of course, that at the time when Ministers were considering the subject at Chequers, nothing had happened in Washington to suggest that any new peace initiative was afoot or that anything more significant was likely than the numerous proposals that had been made in previous weeks, to which the Argentines had always responded negatively.

Even if, assuming it had been possible, British Ministers had been told that discussions had been going on between Washington, Lima and Buenos Aires about the possibility of some new ideas for peace to be put forward with Peruvian blessing, I do not think that they would on that account have refrained from a decision they thought necessary for the security of British forces. They had had three weeks of Argentine diplomatic prevarication. It was widely thought that, if negotiations were ever going to lead to anything, this would be as a result not of conciliatory noises but of direct and heavy military pressure.

To come to a verdict on this subject, it is necessary to bear in mind the military scene as it looked to London at the end of April and beginning of May. The task force still had to face the Argentine air force. The Argentine surface fleet was at sea. Their active submarines posed some threat to British forces. The Argentines were finding it possible to supply the islands regularly by sea. The dangers resulting from the lack of adequate air reconnaissance and air defence for the British Fleet were apparent. How could Ministers in that atmosphere have desisted from authorizing any measure that they thought necessary for the security of their forces?

Given the key part that this incident is said to have played in the diplomatic scene, I cannot refrain from registering my view that the *Belgrano* and its two escorting destroyers, equipped with Exocet missiles, must inherently have been a danger. Apart from their own weapons, they provided useful air guidance for Argentine air attacks on British forces. Their own position and direction at the time of the attack were irrelevant. Following the *Belgrano* sinking, the Argentine Fleet never left port again, which considerably reduced the threat to British forces. Certainly, the *Belgrano* appeared menacing to Admiral Woodward. This is how he has described it subsequently: 'Early on the morning of 2 May all the indications were that the *Veinticinco de Mayo*, the Argentine carrier, and a group of escorts, had slipped past my forward nuclear submarine barrier to the north, while the cruiser *General Belgrano* and her escorts were attempting to complete the pincer movement from the south while outside the Total Exclusion Zone' (TEZ). Some critics seem to think that there was something not quite fair in attacking a ship outside the TEZ. But the purpose of the TEZ and of the earlier Maritime Exclusion Zone was to try to enforce a blockade of the islands. They were not intended, and could not after the 23 April declaration have been taken to have been intended, to limit the inherent right of self-defence of the British forces.

It is something of a calumny on the Argentine forces to allege, as has been done, that they were entirely pacific until we sank the *Belgrano*. The reality is that a large force of Argentine Mirages did their best to sink the *Glamorgan* a day before the attack on the *Belgrano*, and the Argentine authorities had also ordered their frigates to attack the *Hermes*. We also knew of an Argentine plan for a co-ordinated attack on the task force to be conducted by aircraft from the mainland, from carrier-based aircraft and from surface ships equipped with Exocets.

From the discussions I have had subsequently I do not believe that any of those who were responsible for the decision to attack the *Belgrano* hesitated about it at the time or have had any regrets about it since, except of course for the loss of life inseparable from war. I certainly do not think that they need have any doubts on the score of the impact of their decision on the negotiations, which, indeed, continued after the sinking.

Just before he left Washington on that afternoon of Sunday, 2 May, for New York, Pym received a telephone call from Haig stressing the importance of the Peruvian ideas. Pym then asked me to speak to Haig to emphasize that he was of course ready to consider new ideas if they amounted to anything, but what had been put forward so far seemed only vague and indeterminate and provided no basis on which to do business. I spoke accordingly to Haig and reported this by telegram to London less than an hour after the despatch of the first telegram.

At about 20.00 hours Washington time, I was having dinner at home when Haig telephoned. He told me of the attack on the *Belgrano*. It was the first I had heard of it. He went on to speculate very calmly about the effect of this incident on the Argentines. He was not sure about it. He thought I had better come down and have a talk with him as soon as possible the following day.

In New York Pym was seeing Perez de Cuellar, the UN Secretary-General, that evening. The Secretary-General gave him a set of ideas for a negotiated settlement which he also communicated to the Argentines. These ideas covered the usual ground: troop withdrawals, lifting of sanctions and exclusion zone, transitional arrangements, and diplomatic negotiations for a long-term settlement. It is pertinent to note that the Argentine Ambassador to the United Nations continued to discuss these points with the Secretary-General daily from 2 May to 19 May (as did the British Ambassador to the UN, Anthony Parsons), so there can be no question of the *Belgrano* having ditched diplomacy in New York.

Meanwhile, let us see what had been going on in Lima. Much has been alleged about the progress there, in which the Argentines were engaged, before the decision to sink the *Belgrano* was taken at Chequers. The British representative in Lima is said to have been involved in what were regarded as promising talks for a diplomatic solution. Details have even been published in several British papers and quoted in the House of Commons describing the 'red leather' in which the treaty had been bound ready for signature. The truth is less colourful.

On Saturday, 1 May, the British Ambassador to Lima, C. W. Wallace, saw the Peruvian Foreign Minister, Dr Arias Stella, on instructions from London to give an account of the situation in the South Atlantic. Dr Arias Stella asked if there was any way in which Peru could help to break the diplomatic deadlock. He made no specific suggestion, that is to say he advanced no new plan; nor did he give any hint at all that a Peruvian initiative might even be in preparation, let alone in an advanced state.

The following day President Belaunde gave a press conference at 18.00 hours Lima time (midnight London time) – that is, four hours after the *Belgrano* had been sunk, although the Peruvians did not yet know this. He stated, without giving details, that Haig had telephoned him the previous night (1 May) to put to him a seven-point plan. There was as yet no agreement on it but the Argentines were considering it and he hoped to be able to make an announcement about it later that night or the following day. Half an hour later the Peruvian Foreign Minister summoned the British Ambassador to say that the previous day he had, on President Belaunde's instructions, telephoned the Argentine Foreign Minister, Costa Mendez, to urge him to accept the new formula. This had been discussed by Belaunde and Haig and modified as a result of these talks into the seven-point formula. Dr Arias Stella claimed that the formula had the approval of Costa Mendez, that Galtieri had told Belaunde that he was well disposed towards it but that he had his 'senate' to consult and convince. The junta were meeting then to consider the terms and their reply was expected hourly. Arias Stella told Wallace the following day that the previous evening – the evening of 2 May Lima time – the junta had rejected the Peruvian proposal as a result of the torpedoing of the Argentine cruiser. But Arias Stella went on to say that the Argentines had not entirely closed the door.

In my first meeting with Haig on 3 May, he told me that Belaunde had complained bitterly about the torpedoing, which he said had wrecked the chance of peace. He was as sore with the United States as he was with Britain.

Haig told me of his worry that the Argentines might return to the Rio Treaty Organization (OAS) confident that they could get support for sanctions against Britain. The United States would veto it but it would divide the hemisphere between north and south. It was being put about in Buenos Aries that the *Belgrano* had been hit as a result of intelligence passed by American satellites and with the help of American special weapons. Haig feared that, if further military action was taken by the British, American opinion and that of the West generally might become less favourable towards Britain. People might say that the British were overreacting.

I told Haig of the attempts the Argentines had made to sink our ships before the *Belgrano* had been attacked. It could not, therefore, be said that the Argentines had been behaving peacefully. Haig said that it was difficult to know whether hitting the Argentines was the only thing that would bring them to negotiate or whether it made them more inflexible, on which I made the obvious retort that for three weeks we had made no attack upon them and they had shown no flexibility.

America Tries to Avert Argentine Humiliation

Haig asked me to suggest to Mrs Thatcher that she should come forward with some declaration expressing readiness to stop hostilities at a certain time provided the Argentines said they would do the same and undertake to withdraw. I said that the Argentines had had plenty of time to negotiate, and what we could not do at this stage was to let up on the military pressure unless there was a categorical assurance that the Argentines were going to stop military action and leave the islands.

When I saw him later the same day Haig told me that he had just spoken to Belaunde. The Peruvian President had told him that the Argentine Generals Iglesias and Moya had just arrived in Lima from Buenos Aires. Belaunde believed that something really must be done to bring about a ceasefire. He thought that the Argentines would accept the seven-point proposal. Haig insisted that military action must be stopped. He did not think that the Argentines could do anything to prevent the British sinking the whole of their fleet. This would bring about the collapse of any authority in Buenos Aires; the whole of Latin America would be alienated.

I repeated the view that Latin America would not be alienated just because we were prepared to defend our rights by force. After three weeks in which the Argentines had reinforced the islands, London was not in a mood for an armistice just because the Argentines were doing badly militarily. Haig repeated once more his worry about the consequences if the British gave the impression of driving things too far.

Haig followed up this talk by sending Enders round to see me with a document containing the seven-point plan and a suggested ceasefire statement to be made by the British Government. This document began with the phrase: 'Whatever happens militarily there must be a negotiated solution to the Falklands crisis if we are to avoid open-ended hostility and instability.'

London replied to the seven-point plan with amendments that I discussed with Haig at a long session on 5 May. Haig said that the British amendments would be rejected out of hand by Argentina. After a lengthy session with me he produced a new set of points which he asked me to transmit to London. Though these latest proposals presented considerable difficulties for London, the British Government accepted them. The text was transmitted by the United States Government to the Peruvians for onward transmission to Argentina, which turned them down. The Argentine aim at this stage appeared to be to move to the United Nations. The British Government let the Secretary-General know that they could go along with the ideas he had produced for a framework for peace, which, to be sure, were similar to those of the seven-point Peruvian plan.

In a mood of frustration at the failure of his efforts, and exasperated at the way the Latin Americans were being so busy and so apparently benign at the UN, Haig left Washington on 12 May for a European tour. No sooner was he out of the country than Mrs Kirkpatrick got into the act. She managed to convince President Reagan that the Argentines were ready to be forthcoming and persuaded him to telephone the Prime Minister, which he did on 13 May. In deciding to telephone Mrs Thatcher, President Reagan had also been influenced by a conversation he had just had with President Figueiredo of Brazil, who had expressed an eagerness to do whatever he could to bring about a peaceful settlement. I discussed this telephone call afterwards with the National Security Adviser, William Clark. Clark told me how concerned President Reagan was about the worsening Falkland islands situation. The United States had already impaired its relations with the Latin American countries. And there would be serious problems in the Alliance if hostilities became intensified and if there were feelings in Britain that America was not being supportive enough.

During his time abroad Haig kept in touch with me by telephone and I had meetings with the acting Secretary of State, Walter Stoessel, and the Political Director in the State Department, Larry Eagleburger, but the focus of negotiation had moved to New York, where Anthony Parsons was intensely involved in talks with the Secretary-General of the UN.

Parsons and I returned to Chequers for a meeting on Sunday, 16 May, as a result of which a British plan was submitted to the Secretary-General the following day. The main features of this British proposal were:

(1) mutual and balanced withdrawal of forces;
(2) appointment of a UN administrator to administer the islands, in consultation with the elected representatives of the islanders;
(3) negotiations between Britain and Argentina on the future of the islands.

Pym had two conversations with Haig in Brussels on 16 and 17 May. Haig said he thought that the British proposal was fair enough, though he doubted whether the Argentines would accept it. Presumably at Haig's instigation, Stoessel asked me on my return to Washington on 18 May whether, in the likely event of Argentine rejection of the British plan, we would want Haig to come forward with another proposal for negotiation. I said most emphatically not. We had been negotiating for six and a half weeks and it was evident that the Argentines were not prepared to talk on any basis that was acceptable to us. Stoessel interjected that Argentine military leaders could now accept nothing.

Sensing a current in the White House running in favour of some last-minute activity by the President, I called on Clark and reminded him of the President's telephone call to the Prime Minister on 13 May. It had been based on the misapprehension that the Argentines were being very forthcoming compared with the British. Clark, for whom the American epithet 'laid-back' must surely have been invented, ruminated a minute or two before saying that Mrs Kirkpatrick was trying to reach him urgently. He understood that she had some suggestions to make and implied that they might be for some negotiating initiative by the President. I asked him to get in touch with me before doing anything. Neither the slow burr of Clark's language, nor his ever-courteous manner, should be taken for indifference. He is totally involved as the President's man, as dedicated to him in office as he is dependent upon him; so there were no grounds for surprise when he reminded me unhurriedly that Mrs Kirkpatrick was the American Ambassador to the United Nations and had to be listened to by the President and his advisers. I repeated the inappropriateness of yet another American negotiating initiative, and Clark answered that he accepted the position. He said I must rest assured that in the event of recourse to the Security Council we could rely on American support. There was no doubt where the President's sympathies lay. Since Clark was working on the draft of the speech the President was to make to members of Parliament in London on 8 June, I took the opportunity to say how closely any words he uttered on the Falklands before and during his visit to Britain would be listened to.

The Argentine response to the British proposal was to seek changes designed to prejudge the outcome of the negotiations, so that they would lead inexorably to Argentine sovereignty and control, to set aside the elected representatives of the islanders and to enable the Argentine authorities to flood the islands with Argentines. Evidently they were still prevaricating in order to consolidate their position on the islands.

Although the Argentine response to the British proposal was negative, the Americans were still not convinced that this was the end of the negotiating road. On 19 May, Haig telephoned me to say that he thought the plan just advanced by the UN Secretary-General would be something that both London and Argentina could accept. The following day, having listened to a good deal of the House of Commons debate, he rang me to say that the British were well postured. But on 21 May, after our forces had landed on the

Falklands, and on several occasions in the next day or two, he told me how anxious he was about the ultimate outcome; he hoped that the British would seize the first moment of military success to show readiness to negotiate. Otherwise he was fearful of the long-term bitterness in Latin America, and the opportunity for the Soviets to increase their influence there. Notwithstanding these anxieties he assured me once again that the American Government would initiate nothing that might jeopardize British interests.

Haig told me on 22 May that the American Embassy in Buenos Aires had just reported the Argentines as talking of breaking off relations with the United States, one pretext being the military material that Britain was receiving from America. This may partly have promoted a visit he paid me at the Embassy that evening to underline the concern of the Administration over likely developments; over the continued will to fight and the spirit of revanchism that would prevail in Buenos Aires whatever the government in power, unless this could be headed off by British readiness to negotiate now rather than to pursue the conflict to a bitter conclusion. The *New York Times*, incidentally, had that morning published defeatist stories based on official briefing. Haig did not see that our interests would be served by any outcome that left us having to keep a large military force on the islands for an indefinite future subject to attack from the Argentine mainland.

On 24 May, on instructions, I told Haig that the establishment of the British bridgehead in the Falklands was bound to have a major effect on our diplomatic position. We could not in present circumstances consider the idea of British withdrawal from the Falklands or the establishment of an interim administration. We were determined to bring about Argentine withdrawal with the fewest possible casualties and remained interested in serious negotiations. But the Argentines must demonstrate a real change of position by, for instance, indicating a willingness to withdraw within a fixed time-limit.

Haig said that he thought the British attitude was quite understandable. Nevertheless, he felt obliged to point out that there were long-term issues at stake that might well be jeopardized if breadth of vision were not shown at this stage. The dispute had already greatly jeopardized American interests in Latin America. He suggested to me a possible plan involving a ceasefire and withdrawal, a US–Brazilian interim administration (President Figueiredo had made a considerable impact on Washington thinking) and discussions about the future without prior commitment. All this reflected Haig's anxiety about the impending meeting of the Rio Treaty which, he foresaw, would isolate the United States from its hemispheric neighbours. I told Haig immediately, without reference to London, that these ideas would be unacceptable there in current circumstances. Haig repeated his view about the need to keep the Brazilians in play so as to prevent the OAS from getting out of control, which would spell the end of the Inter-American system and the United States would be blamed. It would be a disaster if the outcome of the Falklands crisis was an intensification of Communism and Soviet influence in the American hemisphere. In the long run, the only security for the islands was some agreement in which the United States participated, but it would be impossible to get an American guarantee for a return to the status quo.

I reminded Haig how often he had assured me that this would not be another Suez. Considerable sacrifices had already been made by Britain and these must not be rendered vain by a premature termination of our task. We recognized the importance of America's relations with its Latin American neighbours but Haig should not overlook the possible risk to relations between the United States, Britain and Western Europe generally. Haig accepted all this and repeated that he did not want to do anything that would cause difficulties for us but rather wanted to act in concert with us. He would like to think that a joint appeal by the American and Brazilian Governments to both sides could be devised in advance so as to make it acceptable to Britain.

Later the same day, Haig telephoned to say that the President supported Britain solidly. In order to keep the idea of a negotiation going, he sent Pym a further message saying that the United States would be prepared to provide a battalion to ensure no violation of any interim agreement on the Falklands. He asked the British Government to consider a scheme submitted by Brazil in New York for withdrawal and an interim administration, with the addition, so Haig suggested, of a US–Brazilian peace-keeping force. He followed this up with a plea to London that, when we had reached the highest point of military pressure, we should offer a magnanimous proposal to bring military activity to an end.

By this time British forces had been engaged in hazardous operations, and the bridgehead had been established at San Carlos. The heavy Argentine air attacks marking their national day on 25 May heightened the tension in Washington almost as acutely as in London. On instructions from the Prime Minister and Pym, I rubbed it home in Washington that we were determined to repossess the Falklands and to reinstate British administration and only thereafter would we consider future developments, though we acknowledged the desirability eventually of having some kind of international security arrangement involving the Americans.

In frequent conversations with me during these days Haig confessed to his nightmare that Argentina, whatever the immediate military outcome, would remain in a state of war with us. He hoped that we would win militarily and soon but that in doing so we would offer some proposal which would help our own, and the United States', long-term interests in the American hemisphere.

His concerns were obviously being fuelled by the 'latino lobby' in the State Department, which briefed the press on the evening of 25 May that Haig had sent Pym a message urging Britain not to try to crush the Argentines and predicting that the Argentines would look for a scapegoat for a British victory, and that scapegoat would probably be the United States.

On 26 May, the UN Security Council unanimously adopted a resolution calling on the Secretary-General to renew his mission of good offices with a view to negotiating a ceasefire between Britain and Argentina. Perez de Cuellar thereupon asked the two sides to provide their 'bottom line'. Haig urged us not to give an answer until after the Rio Treaty meeting due to begin in Washington on 27 May.

I gave him Pym's reply to his message calling for a magnanimous gesture on our part. Pym stressed that, with the establishment of the British bridgehead in the Falklands, it would no longer be realistic to ask people in Britain to accept the ideas of an interim administration or mutual withdrawal from the Falkland Islands. Pym wondered whether some of Haig's ideas, and particularly his offer of a battalion, might be used at a somewhat later stage, namely after repossession of the islands, the restoration of British administration and consultation with the islanders about their wishes for the future.

The Rio Treaty meeting was characterized by a series of venomous attacks on the United States for its support of Britain. Haig made a stalwart speech and, while emphasizing the historic value of the inter-American system, made it clear that Argentina had rejected every plan put forward since its invasion of the Falklands. Haig told me afterwards that, whatever the pressures I might feel under, they were nothing compared with the five standing ovations against him that had taken place during that day.

Haig soon began to show considerable concern at what had been described to him as a hardening of the British attitude. He sketched out a possible framework agreement which included the idea of an international umbrella organization to supervise the local government, thereby eliminating the colonial tag, and to consider the ultimate status of the islands. It was an essential feature of this latest American initiative that it should be launched before the final defeat of the Argentine forces.

It contained the following elements:
(1) With the end of fighting and the defeat of the Argentine forces there would be a British military administration.
(2) This military administration would give way to a form of self-government in accordance with the principles of Article 73 of the UN charter. This system of government would be such as to remove the colonialist tag which a return to the status quo would mean. The establishment of this self-government would be accompanied by some declaration of principles by which the country would be run.
(3) This local government would be subject to an international umbrella which would also have a small international force. The umbrella coun-

tries would include the United States and probably Brazil. The Argentines would probably have a liaison officer. The terms of reference of the umbrella group would provide for it to ensure that the local government was being carried out in accordance with the principles that had been enunciated and to provide for security.

(4) The umbrella group would also have responsibility for considering the ultimate status of the islands. There would be no cut-off date for this and, if no agreement had been reached, the arrangements of self-government and the umbrella would continue.

Haig did not think that the Brazilians, or any other Latin American country, would join in a plan if it came after a humiliating defeat of the Argentines. He asked for a response to his plan by 31 May. He underlined yet again the absolute priority of remaining in lock-step with the British. But he could not conceal his concern about the deteriorating scene in the South Atlantic.

The mood of anxiety in Washington was reflected in the decision taken by the President to telephone the Prime Minister again. This call took place on 31 May. Reagan's purpose seemed to be not only to register concern about Latin American opinion, but to float the idea of another American peace initiative. The Prime Minister telephoned me subsequently to ask me to see Clark at the White House and ensure that the President and he understood the British attitude. On 1 June, I called on Clark and made clear, at Mrs Thatcher's request, that Britain, having negotiated in good faith for weeks, during which time the Argentines had shown no sign of being ready to talk business, was not prepared now, when we were back in the islands after considerable sacrifice, simply to pull out and make way for an umbrella or contact group including countries from Latin America.

Clark said that the President was worried about the considerable damage already done to America's relations with Latin America. In the long term there had to be a settlement about the islands. The President, therefore, thought that there would be value in having Brazil alongside the United States in an attempt at negotiation, but this would not be possible if Brazil thought that the British were insisting on unconditional surrender and the humiliation of Argentina. Clark also mentioned American fears that the Soviet Union would use the crisis to increase their influence in Latin America generally and in Argentina in particular.

Later in the day I had two conversations with Haig in which we went over much of the old ground. He was leaving for Europe the following day with the President. He asked me to keep in close touch with the State Department during his absence. He said that the President would want to discuss with the Prime Minister during his visit to Britain ways of trying to mend fences with Latin America and how to limit Soviet opportunities to exploit the aftermath of the crisis.

Nothing assuaged the American concern at this stage – that is to say at the end of May and the beginning of June – about the dire consequences that would flow from overwhelming military defeat inflicted on the Argentines. This sentiment was reflected in a hand-wringing editorial in the *Washington Post*. I conveyed to London as best I could the evidence of a growing gap between the resolute attitude there and the mood in Washington favouring a soft line by us towards Argentina. There was much talk of magnanimity and Sir Winston Churchill's name was pleaded in aid, upon which I rejoined that Churchill had not talked of magnanimity until after victory had been achieved.

The prospect of a bloody battle for Port Stanley heightened tension at the United Nations, where the Latinos managed to get a resolution introduced into the Security Council calling for an immediate ceasefire and withdrawal.

The President and Haig left for Europe on 2 June with the widespread expectation that, at the meetings he would have with the Prime Minister during the Versailles Summit at the weekend and in London the following week, the President would urge magnanimity on the British Government. This was certainly the tone of much American press comment at the time. However, in an interview which President Reagan gave to European journalists shortly before his departure for Europe he said that it would be presumptuous of him to insist that the British seek a negotiated settlement: 'I know that both sides have lost men. But England responded to a threat that all of us must oppose and that is the idea that armed aggression can succeed in the world today.'

On 4 June, the Prime Minister and the President talked alone in Paris. Mrs Thatcher thanked him for his help. Haig and Pym met separately at the same time.

Even at this stage, the Americans had still not abandoned hope that there could be some negotiated settlement before the defeat and surrender of the Argentine forces. Picking up reports of a new intervention by the UN Secretary-General for a ceasefire, Stoessel and Enders got in touch with the British Chargé d'Affaires in Washington. They asked for our views on the feasibility of yet one more attempt by the Americans to instil reason into the Argentines. The Chargé d'Affaires left them in no doubt that this was not the time for new proposals and that it was up to the Argentines to give clear evidence of an intention to withdraw immediately.

While meetings were taking place in Europe, and Israel was invading the Lebanon, the diplomatic spotlight and headlines were momentarily off the Falklands, where the British forces were advancing on Port Stanley. Contrary to American fears of a major battle, this was avoided and the Argentine forces surrendered on 14 June.

America's Role: Conclusion

Undeniably, the ceaseless diplomatic efforts that the United States made from early April did not achieve their main purpose, which was to bring about a settlement that avoided bloodshed and humiliation for either side. But from the British angle, these prolonged negotiations brought advantages. During the considerable time that elapsed between the despatch of the task force from Britain and its readiness to repossess the islands, there was a need for something to fill the diplomatic vacuum. There were positive advantages in Haig's to-ings and fro-ings and frequent proposals. Without them, Argentine intransigence would not have been exposed, and without this exposure the American decision to give Britain support would probably not have come when it did or have been so categorical. So I think that people were wrong at the time who saw the issue for us simply as a choice between diplomatic negotiations that would be undesirable because they could not give us everything and a battle that would be bound to be hazardous.

Before Haig's revelations to me of his visits to Buenos Aires I did not think that it was self-evident that the junta was beyond reason. Even when that became apparent, it was essential if we were to persuade the Americans of our reasonableness and secure their support that we should show ourselves willing, and indeed be willing, to negotiate. To put it the other way round, I believe that, if we had been completely intransigent, if we had treated Haig's ideas, or the Peruvian initiative, or any of the other proposals, as sell-outs that were not worth considering, we might well not have had the Americans on our side.

I have no doubt that Haig's role was crucial. He perceived that a principle was involved. He also saw how close a bearing the crisis had on the future of the Atlantic Alliance. He took us at all times into his confidence, even when this involved thinking aloud, and we gained greatly from this.

But although Haig dominated American policy on this issue he never succeeded in eliminating everyone from the wings, where indeed there were always plenty of people lurking and eager to seize the centre of the stage and play a different role from his. The influence of these pro-Latinos may well have encouraged the Argentines in their intransigence, just as it may have emboldened them to take their impetuous decision to invade; but it is impossible to be categorical about this.

The nature of the American Government makes it very difficult to have one clear-cut and comprehensive fount of policy. If Haig had been the sort of character who was easy in accepting compromises, self-effacing and ready to yield to pressure and capable of adopting tactics of lying in wait and stalking, so useful in the Washington jungle, he might have reduced the internecine strife that bedevilled the Administration, but he would not then have been the person to have given the lead he did, which gave such a decisive direction to American policy.

My overall conclusions about the negotiations and the role of the United States and its Secretary of State are these. First, had the Argentines accepted the proposals frequently offered to them they would have secured something and would have been better off than they were by choosing the alternative outcome of military confrontation leading to surrender. Secondly, it does not follow from this that the British Government's interests would have suffered from the sort of settlement we were prepared to accept at different stages in the prolonged negotiation. What we were ready to agree to would, I believe, have safeguarded the essential interests of the British Government and the islanders.

Thirdly, the sinking of the *Belgrano* did not thwart a promising new negotiating initiative, though the Argentines have found it convenient to make this allegation. The British Government knew nothing of any new initiative when they authorized the sinking; and there was nothing to suggest at the time that the Argentines were any readier to negotiate than they had been during the previous month. There were good military reasons to authorize the attack. After the sinking of the *Belgrano*, the Argentines continued to show as much, or as little, interest in negotiations as at any other time.

Fourthly, American support was not something that was inevitable; it could not have been taken for granted and could have been lost at any time had we shown complete intransigence in negotiation.

Fifthly, some measure of the significance of American support for Britain over the Falklands can be gathered by imagining what it would have been like for Britain to have been detached from its most powerful ally as we were at Suez. From my discussions with service leaders since the events, I conclude that it is difficult to exaggerate the difference that America's support made to the military outcome.

BRITAIN'S ECONOMIC PERFORMANCE SINCE 1979; AND RELATIONS WITH THE EUROPEAN COMMUNITY

Britain's Economic Performance since 1979: Relations with the EC

On 2 June 1979, *The Economist* published the text of the confidential Valedictory Despatch I wrote from Paris at the end of my term as Ambassador there (it is reproduced here on p. 143). My despatch of 1979 had two themes: the economic decline of Britain over the previous quarter of a century compared with France and Germany; and the contribution to this decline made by the foreign policy pursued by British Governments during the same period. The question I now wish to answer is how far there has been a change in either respect since Mrs Thatcher's Government came to power in 1979. Because the decline was aggravated in the early years of our membership of the European Community by Britain's unpopularity with its fellow members, I shall go on to examine our current relations with the Community.

The following are among those whom I have consulted personally in making this assessment of Britain's economic performance:

Sir Geoffrey Chandler, formerly director-general, National Economic Development Office (NEDO); director, Industry Year 1986
Sir James Cleminson, formerly president of Confederation of British Industry (CBI); now chairman, British Overseas Trade Board
Sir John Egan, chairman, Jaguar
Richard Freeman, chief economist, ICI
Michael Hart, manager of the Foreign and Colonial Investment Trust
Sir John Harvey-Jones, chairman, ICI
Quinton Hazell, formerly chairman of the Economic Planning Council of the West Midlands
Sir Alexander Jarratt, chairman, Employment Policy Committee, CBI, since 1983; chairman, Smiths Industries; deputy chairman, Midland Bank
Robert Malpas, director, ICI, 1975–8; managing director of BP since 1983
Dr John White, group managing director, BBA Group

Sir Robert Armstrong, Secretary of the Cabinet and Head of the Civil Service
Nicholas Bayne, United Kingdom Representative to the OECD
Sir Julian Bullard, British Ambassador to West Germany
Sir Terence Burns, Chief Economic Adviser to the Treasury
Sir Michael Butler, formerly British Ambassador to the European Communities
Sir Peter Carey, formerly Permanent Secretary, Department of Industry; subsequently connected with merchant banking and industry as a director
Sir James Fawcett, formerly President, European Commission of Human Rights
Sir John Fretwell, British Ambassador to France
Sir David Hannay, British Ambassador to the European Communities

Sir Brian Hayes, Permanent Secretary, Department of Trade and Industry
Robin Renwick, Assistant Under-Secretary of State, Foreign and Commonwealth Office
Kate Timms, Counsellor, British Embassy, Paris

The Rt Hon. Kenneth Clarke MP, Paymaster-General and Minister for Employment
The Rt Hon. the Earl Jellicoe, chairman, Davy Corporation; formerly chairman, British Overseas Trade Board and of Tate & Lyle and Leader of the House of Lords
The Rt Hon. Roy Jenkins MP, formerly Home Secretary and Chancellor of the Exchequer and President, European Commission
The Rt Hon. Cecil Parkinson MP, formerly Secretary of State for Trade and Industry
The Rt Hon. John Smith MP, Opposition Spokesman for Trade and Industry
The Rt Hon. Lord Young of Graffham, Secretary of State for Employment

John Edmonds, general secretary, General, Municipal, Boilermakers and Allied Trades Union
Eric Hammond, general secretary, Electrical, Electronic, Telecommunications and Plumbing Union
Gavin Laird, general secretary, Amalgamated Engineering Union
David Lambert, president, National Union of Hosiery and Knitwear Workers
David Lea, assistant general secretary, TUC
Norman Willis, general secretary, TUC

The Rt Hon. the Earl of Drogheda, director, Times Newspaper Holdings Ltd
Lucy Hodges, formerly Education Correspondent of *The Times*
Anatole Kaletsky, *Financial Times*
Robert Taylor, Labour Correspondent, *Observer*

Professor Alan Budd, London Business School

Vicomte Davignon, formerly member and Vice-President of the Committee of the European Communities
Jean François-Poncet, Senator; formerly French Foreign Minister
Elisabeth Guigou, Conseiller Technique to the French President
Jean-Claude Paye, Secretary-General, OECD

Dr Wilhelm Christians, chairman, Deutsche Bank, Düsseldorf
Professor Horst Ehmke, chairman, Social Democratic Party Committee on

Foreign Affairs and Defence in the Bundestag; formerly West German Minister of Science and Technology
Detlev Rohwedder, chairman, Hoesch; formerly West German Minister of Economic Affairs
Dr Jürgen Ruhfus, State Secretary, West German Ministry of Foreign Affairs

I do not claim that these people represent a complete cross-section of British or Continental opinion, or that they accurately reflect the political or social composition of the country. Nor do I assert that this has been anything in the nature of a comprehensive enquiry. It has been an attempt by someone who is not a journalist and who is no longer a diplomat to form and delineate an impression with the help of a piecemeal and personal poll.

Statistics

Most of the following statistical material can be compared with that given in my Valedictory Despatch. Some new tables are provided, for example on fixed capital formation, to highlight our present economic performance against our recent past and contrast it with that of France and West Germany. The tables are based on statistics provided by the Organization for Economic Co-operation and Development, the Central Statistical Office, the Department of Trade and Industry, the Department of Employment and ICI.

Table 1   Real GDP (average annual percentage increases)

	1960–8	1968–73	1973–9	1979–84	1985
Britain	3.1	3.2	1.5	0.6	3.2
France	5.4	5.9	3.1	1.1	1.2
West Germany	4.1	4.9	2.3	0.9	2.4

Table 2   Comparison of Size of GDP (calculated by purchasing-power parities; Britain = 100)

	1979	1981	1984
Britain	100	100	100
France	109	114	111
West Germany	127	134	129

Table 3 Real GDP Per Head (average annual percentage increases)

	1960–8	1968–73	1973–9	1979–84
Britain	2.4	2.8	1.5	0.5
France	4.2	5.0	2.6	0.6
West Germany	3.2	4.0	2.5	1.0

Table 4 Comparison of GDP Per Head (calculated by purchasing-power parities; Britain = 100)

	1979	1981	1984
Britain	100	100	100
France	114	119	114
West Germany	118	123	119

The figures in Tables 1 to 4 lead to the following conclusions. First the gap between the annual rate of growth in Britain compared with France and Germany has narrowed in the years 1979–84. Secondly, as regards these growth figures there was a decline in GDP in Britain in the years 1979–81, whereas growth continued in those years in France and Germany. Since 1981 GDP has grown faster in Britain than in France or in Germany. The figures for 1985 are particularly encouraging. Thirdly, over the course of the five years from 1979 both France and Germany increased their lead over Britain in the size of their GDP by 2 per cent each. To be more specific, Britain lost ground sharply over the first two years and has been catching up from 1981 onwards. Fourthly, in terms of GDP per head, Britain was in virtually the same position in 1984 relative to France and Germany as it was in 1979.

Table 5 Productivity: Output Per Person Employed (average annual percentage increases)

	1960–8	1968–73	1973–9	1979–84	1985
Britain	2.7	3.0	1.3	1.7	2.2
France	4.9	4.7	2.8	1.4	1.4
West Germany	4.2	4.1	2.9	1.5	1.7

Table 5 shows that Britain has achieved stronger growth in productivity over the last five years than either France or Germany, for the first time since 1960. This has been achieved, however, at the cost of higher unemployment rates than in either of the other two countries, as shown in Table 6.

Table 6 Standardized[a] Unemployment Rates (as percentage of labour force)

	1979	1980	1982	1984	1985	Average 1979–84
Britain	5.1	6.6	11.4	13.0	13.2	9.75
France	5.9	6.3	8.1	9.7	10.1	7.6
West Germany	3.2	3.0	6.1	8.5	8.6	5.5

[a] Adjustments have been made to national statistics to make them compatible with one another.

The above figures suggest one obvious conclusion: that the greater productivity Britain has undoubtedly achieved in recent years has led, not so much to expansion, as to lay-offs. The Government would not, of course, deny the scale of jobs lost since 1979. But they would argue that the degree of shedding was an index of the overmanning which had been indulged in for so long. Industry could only become competitive by laying off excessive manpower.

Less controversial are the figures for industrial disputes (Britain had 2,080 in 1979, 840 in 1985) and inflation (see Table 7).

Table 7 Consumer Prices (percentage increases from previous year)

	1979	1980	1982	1984	1985	Average 1979–84
Britain	13.4	18.0	8.6	5.0	6.1	8.5
France	10.8	13.6	11.8	7.4	5.8	7.4
West Germany	4.1	5.5	5.3	2.4	2.2	4.0

Table 8 Unit Labour Costs in Manufacturing (average annual percentage increases)

	1968–73	1973–9	1979–84	1985
Britain	7.9	18.6	7.3	4.85
France	5.2	10.7	9.5	2.7
West Germany	6.9	4.8	2.9	−1.0

Table 8 shows that, in manufacturing, Britain has gained competitiveness against France but has continued to lose it against Germany since 1979. It is also worth noting that the average annual increase for unit labour costs for this period for the United States was only 4.7 per cent, the same as the

OECD average, while unit labour costs in Japan fell each year by an average of 2 per cent. This table helps to illustrate the dilemma for British industry. Increases in real earnings help to restore the incentives given to the British labour force, which had fallen behind in the 1970s compared with its European neighbours. But these increases can be self-defeating, if they reduce Britain's external competitiveness.

I have found foreign observers surprised that unit labour costs should have risen so much in Britain in a period when the power of the unions has been reduced by both legislation and the impact of the recession and high unemployment. I know that some members of the British Government believed that, faced with the alternative of more people out of work but an increase in wages for those employed, or more at work but with some sacrifice in pay, the trade unions would choose the second. But they did not. Kenneth Clarke, Minister for Employment, points out that, despite the decrease in inflation, earnings over the past three years have been increasing at twice the rate of the rise in GDP. It has also been made clear to me that these high unit labour costs are seen by the British Government as a threat to the competitiveness of British industry. There is a tendency for management to reach a going rate for wage increases regardless of the performance of the company. Given such high wage rates, management are inclined to see cost-effectiveness in terms of the reduction of the labour force. The figures in Table 9 show the large increase in wages in British manufacturing industry compared with those in France and Germany.

Table 9 Average Gross Hourly Earnings in Manufacturing Industry (pounds per hour at current exchange rates)

	April 1979	October 1983	Percentage change
Britain	1.89	3.13	+66
France	2.09	2.82	+35
West Germany	3.15	3.91	+24

Table 10 Share of Manufactured Goods Exported by OECD Countries (percentage shares, at current prices and exchange rates)

	1966	1979	1984
Britain	12	9	7
France	8	10	8
West Germany	18	19	17

The figures in Table 10 do not reassure one that Britain has held its share of exports of manufactures since 1979.

Table 11   Passenger Cars Per Thousand Inhabitants

	1977	1984
Britain	255	312
France	314	360
West Germany	326	412

According to Table 11, Britain has caught the French up a little in car-ownership but fallen further behind the Germans.

Jaguar, incidentally, were producing 14,000 cars per annum in 1979. This had increased to 40,000 by 1985. However, BMW are producing vehicles at the rate of 400,000 per annum. These simple figures show both the great recent improvement in Jaguar and also the enormous distance the British motor-car industry has to go to catch up with its Continental competitors.

I have received frequent complaints from industrial managers that the incidence of taxation is heavier for them than it is for industry in France and Germany, thereby impairing their competitiveness. Table 12 gives the figures on direct taxation.

Table 12   Direct Taxes on Corporate and Quasi-corporate Enterprises (as percentage of contribution to GDP)

	1975	1979	1983
Britain	5.0	5.5	8.8
France	5.0	5.0	5.2
West Germany	2.1	3.1	2.8

On the face of it Table 12 bears out the managerial complaints, just as it explains the cry for increased capital allowances for new investment. But it relates in the main to corporation tax or its foreign equivalent; it does not cover social security contributions, which are higher in France and Germany than in Britain. The leap in the direct tax burden on British companies between 1979 and 1983 may well reflect the impact of North Sea Oil. On the basis of comparable data I am not convinced that British industry has a justified grievance on this score of taxation. I am also impressed by a recent report by the OECD on the difficulties of making international comparisons of corporate tax burdens, and on the dangers of drawing conclusions from them about competitiveness.

If Mrs Thatcher and others who have had responsibility for the British economy since 1979 were to be asked if they were satisfied or disappointed with the results so far achieved, they might well admit that the turnaround is taking longer than they had reckoned; and they might plead in extenuation the long period during which our economy has been in decline. There were worries about keeping up with the Germans even as early as the middle of the last century;[1] but measures of economic performance such as GDP were not then available – to guide or depress. Figure 1 shows the long-term percentage growth of GDP in the main industrial countries.

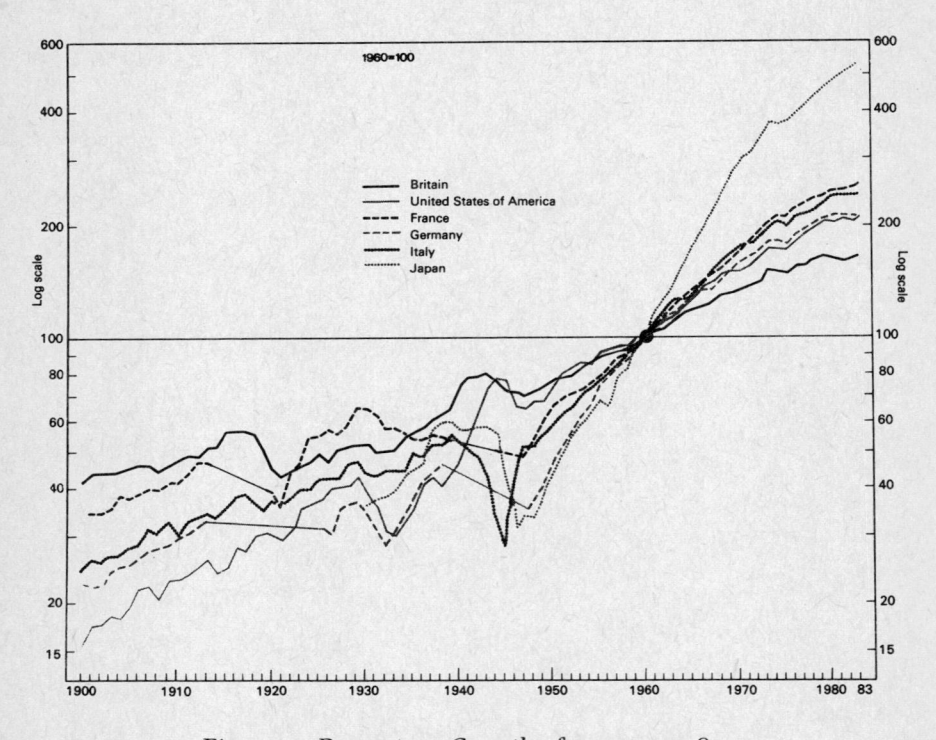

Figure 1   Percentage Growth of GDP 1900–83

Figure 1 is taken from Thelma Liesner's book *Economic Statistics 1900–1983*.[2] It demonstrates features that have to be taken into account in any discussion of current trends. First, Britain has been the industrial country

[1] *Striking a Balance: the Role of the Board of Trade 1886–1986* (Her Majesty's Stationery Office, 1986).
[2] Economist Publications, 1985.

which has persistently had the slowest rate of growth throughout this century; this obviously aggravates the problem of reversing the trend in a short period of time. Secondly, in the second half of this century Britain's GDP has been growing relatively well compared with the first half: the annual rate of growth 1950–83 has been 2.5 per cent, compared with just over 1 per cent in the period 1900–38. Nevertheless Britain has done much less well than either France or Germany (and the other industrial countries).

Attention might also be drawn to another inheritance from the past – capital formation – which is bound to affect present-day growth. Mrs Liesner's book gives figures set out in Table 13.

Table 13 Fixed Capital Formation as a Percentage of GDP

	1950	1970	1980
Britain	13	21	18
France	17	23	22
West Germany	20	24	22

For thirty years, therefore, as Table 13 shows, we have been falling behind France and Germany in the basic requirements for growth – the provision of plant and machinery, buildings and infrastructure. It is fair to say, however, that the Bank of England *Quarterly Bulletin* in June 1986 arrives at rather more favourable comparative figures for Britain over the past three decades than those given by Mrs Liesner. However, the *Bulletin* figures are based on somewhat different criteria; for example, they exclude housing from the total national capital formation data, use Gross National Product (GNP) rather than GDP and show figures at current prices rather than constant prices. Nonetheless, the *Bulletin* estimates that the net capital stock of manufacturing industry in Britain contracted by 2.75 per cent between 1979 and 1985.

I do not have any confident figures from official sources about future trends. But Table 14 (see p. 120) sets out forecasts published by *Time* magazine in July 1986 on the basis of estimates by their European Board, which comprises six distinguished economists: Samuel Brittan, Guido Carli, Jean-Marie Chevalier, Herbert Giersch, Nils Lundgren and Hans Mast.

Table 14 hardly presents a rosy outlook for Britain – at any rate as seen by a group of non-official specialists.

Table 14 Forecasts Concerning Growth, Inflation and Unemployment
(percentages)

	Growth Change in real GNP (year on year)		Inflation Change in CPI[a] (Dec. over Dec.)		Unemployment Proportion of labour force (year-end)	
	1986	1987	1986	1987	1986	1987
Britain	1.8	2.6	2.0	3.5	13.3	13.0
France	2.5	2.8	2.6	2.5	11.0	11.0
West Germany	4.3	3.3	0.0	3.0	8.5	7.5

[a] Consumer Price Index.

Causes and Consequences

Moving from figures to generalizations I would like to bring up to date certain comparisons between Britain and our neighbours which I drew seven years ago. At that time I made a number of assertions based on the way Britain looked to someone who had been living abroad. Now that I have been back in Britain for some time and have been more closely involved in what is going on, I perhaps focus differently on underlying causes and likely consequences.

Manufacturing Versus Service Industry

A fruitless debate has raged in the past few years over the importance of manufacturing industry compared with service industry and tourism. The British Government are partly responsible for this. Because Britain's manufacturing industry has declined they have sought to make a virtue of it by saying that this can be well compensated for by the increase of service industry and tourism which in any case are more labour-intensive. Government sources rubbished the Aldington Report,[3] which tried to draw attention to the serious consequences of the reducion of our manufacturing base. They pooh-poohed the idea that the weakness of our manufacturing industry constituted a grave threat to the country's economic and political stability, as the Aldington Report had stated. What in fact the Government were doing was putting on record their determination to resist pressure to discriminate in favour of manufacturing industry in any policy of financial support. While

[3] *Report from the House of Lords Committee on Balance of Trade in Manufactures*, Ref. 238/I.

understanding the argument intellectually I cannot see how the Government can be sanguine about the continued decline of manufacturing industry (which still employs over 5 million people in Britain – though this is up to 1.5 million less than in 1979). What matters is wealth creation, the production of the means to pay for essential services (for example, health, £17 billion per annum; education, £14 billion per annum; or defence, £18 billion per annum) and imports. Obviously service industry and tourism can make an important contribution and they are bound to grow; they are also areas in which jobs are likely to increase, whereas in manufacturing industry technology will increasingly drive out employment. The real question is by how much they can take the place of manufactures, which over a long period of time have declined more in Britain than in any other developed country, so much so that Sir John Harvey-Jones, chairman of ICI, has described them as 'an endangered species'. There is no way in which services or tourism can be increased sufficiently to pay even for the scale of imports required to maintain our standard of life. You only have to live in London to realize that we can hardly cope with the number of tourists who already come here. To give one example: the total earnings from tourism at the present time amount to about half the value of the goods produced by a single manufacturing company, ICI.

Roy Jenkins points out that '64 per cent of our labour force is already employed in services, which produce only one-quarter of our overseas trading income. A little more than 20 per cent still employed in manufacturing industry must produce the rest.' The same dire note is struck by Lord Jellicoe, chairman of Davy Corporation, who has had a distinguished career in both government and industry. 'I remain profoundly worried about the Government's attitude – or at least the attitude of some influential members of the Government – towards manufacturing industry, as evidenced by their contemptuous dismissal of the Aldington Report,' he says. In his diagnosis of the cause of our decline relative to that of other West European countries I hear the same dirge as I have listened to so frequently from others – too many of our national leaders have shunned manufacturing industry for far too long. Lord Jellicoe dismisses as absurd the idea that we might be able to jog along comfortably into the twenty-first century relying on our service industries. These will not be able to survive, in his view, unless they have a sound manufacturing base to service. Nor can they possibly fill the gap left by declining oil earnings.

The Government's Role

Roy Jenkins believes that the Government are standing back too much from industry. In his experience they do so more than any other government in the European Community. 'This totally arm's-length approach in the relationship between government and industry,' he concludes, 'is something that no other comparable government contemplates to the extent that we do. It is not producing good results for British industry and it is a recipe for a further decline in Britain's position in the Western world.'

The present British Government have a penchant for saying one thing and doing another, as in this hands-off policy towards industry. In practice, they have done much to create the climate for better industrial relations; they have initiated vocational training programmes and provided help for small businesses, such as the Business Expansion Scheme. They can claim that 140,000 more new businesses have been started up than closed down between 1980 and 1985. The Government are committed to spending £3 billion in 1986–7 to promote employment and training for enterprise. Indeed they have appointed a Cabinet Minister with responsibility, not simply for employment, but for enterprise. Lord Young acknowledges the shortcomings of industry: 'Most people see it in terms of "us and them", with each side doing its best to do down the other,' a gap between management and the shop floor that is not, as he points out, to be found in Japanese industry.

I asked someone who has been prominent in both government and industry what he thought. Sir Peter Carey, former Permanent Secretary at the Department of Trade and Industry and now a leading industrialist, said that over the past seven years the Government had not done enough to arrest our industrial and economic decline. The pace may have lessened but if it continues as at present, particularly in respect of our manufacturing industry, 'our standard of living will be found to fall in relation to our competitors since service industry cannot alone fill the gap. This in time will threaten our social stability and democratic system.' But he does not think that this is necessarily irreversible, 'provided that Government, management and unions accept, over a period of several decades, that wealth-creation must be the prime objective, and that Government of whatever party will determine the tax structure and influence the exchange and interest rates with this objective primarily in mind'.

Autres Moeurs: The Lessons of Japan

Although it was outside the scope of my enquiry in 1979 and I did not therefore deal with it in my Valedictory Despatch I have been unable this time to ignore the Japanese example because so many people have talked to me about it. The Japanese claim to have solved the problem of traditional industries such as textiles, shipping and steel, which have been rendered uncompetitive by low-cost producers. They have moved into new regions requiring high technology. This has been made possible, not simply by the skill of management, but by the restraint of shareholders, who in Japan are apparently prepared to forego immediate profits in return for the assurance of long-term development. It has been put to me that, in contrast, the objective of private industry in Britain is maximum profit in the shortest possible time, or in some instances maximum cash-flow; the focus is on the bottom line, whereas in Japan it is on the prospects for a bigger return in the future. This is but one manifestation of the varying nature of capitalism in different countries. Indeed, I have been struck by the insistence of those on the left of the political spectrum on the lack of uniformity of capitalism and the need for Britain, even at this late juncture of its industrial history, to choose the right model: that is to say, the Swedish method, involving participation and the absence of barriers between management and the workforce, rather than the American model, which is seen as confrontational between the two sides. I suppose that the practice of co-determination (*Mitbestimmung*) in West Germany is a good deal closer to the Swedish than the American system; but it is not one to which the other members of the European Community have felt drawn. Nobody thinks we could imitate Japan.

The Japanese success story seems to haunt all sections of our society, not simply those who are specialists in industrial management or the application of robots to the assembly line. Certainly I found this to be so in the trade union movement. Like many others, David Lambert, president of the National Union of Hosiery and Knitwear Workers, has been impressed by the Japanese, and he is critical of what he describes as the short-term views of British management towards both technology and new investment. He has given an example from his industry of the greater flexibility of the Japanese compared with the British: they have introduced a new technology for cutting fabric which greatly improves productivity and therefore competitiveness. Instances of the greater success of the Japanese at managing industry in this country compared with the British themselves were provided by Eric Hammond, the general secretary of the Electrical, Electronic, Telecommunications and Plumbing Union. He described the failure of a joint GEC–Hitachi Electronics venture in South Wales. After GEC withdrew, Hitachi carried on alone to such effect that within two years their productivity was equal to that of a Japanese factory. In the process, Hitachi had insisted on dealing with one union instead of the seven operating under the previous joint venture. Toshiba had achieved a similar result on their own in the same way in Plymouth, after the failure of a joint venture with Rank.

Another trade union leader, John Edmonds, general secretary of the General, Municipal, Boilermakers and Allied Trades Union, has spoken to me of the Japanese managerial skill in handling the workforce in this country. He told me of a wholly owned Japanese firm in South Wales which produces television equipment. The management took great care in selecting people for employment; they did not expect to find them technically qualified when they joined, so they provided the necessary training for them; they watched over the workforce continually, provided for career development and exercised quality control at every phase of manufacture. Faults were traced back to source. The workforce may find the degree of supervision irksome but they put up with this for the benefit of the high wages, which are 20 per cent above the going rate for the area. Compared with the Japanese, British management, in Edmonds's view, lacks conviction.

Unemployment

One of the most intense convictions that I have found, and it is held across party lines, is that the present scale of unemployment is intolerable, for reasons of both morality and expedience, and that we cannot put up indefinitely with such a scale of unemployment, which is a good deal worse than that of any of our major European partners. Again, I did not even mention this problem in the 1979 despatch because it was so much less acute then than it is now. I must confess to having been startled by the vehemence of the recent strictures on this subject by Samuel Brittan, an economist who has by no means been unsympathetic to many of the present Government's objectives. 'Unemployment', he has written, '*cannot* [his emphasis] be allowed to deteriorate at its present rate. It is no longer good enough to hope that a growth of jobs upturn will come next year. There have been too many "next years".' Brittan says that one can argue until the cows come home whether persistently rising unemployment is due to too much Government spending or to too little spending, to the social security or housing systems or to bureaucratic hindrances on business. When companies are in trouble they lay off people; when they are doing well they do not take on more staff but pay those in employment more. 'The insiders are favoured at the expense of the outsiders,' Brittan complains, adding, 'I would support any of a wide variety of measures to make pay-setting more employment-promoting.'

I have asked many industrialists why those who have money to invest do not create new, or enlarge existing, industrial plants in this country, thereby providing increased employment, rather than placing the money elsewhere, for example in portfolio investment in the United States. The answer I have invariably received is that it is both easier and more profitable to invest overseas. I have been told that in Japan investment in manufacturing industry will bring a return 10 per cent higher than the investment of a similar sum in financial assets. In Britain there is no such premium. Dr John White, group managing director of BBA Group, was quite frank in explaining the dilemma to me. His business makes automated components. His plant in Düsseldorf has a per-capita rate of productivity 30 per cent higher than a plant in Britain making the same product with similar machinery. Why, he asked, should I invest in Britain rather than add to my capacity in Germany? He, like other manufacturers, was critical of the Government's taxation policy, which he thinks does not provide enough incentive for new investment.

The present Government's attitude is well known. It is not a question of not caring. They do not think it is the business of Government to create jobs, or to provide Government money for the creation of jobs. As a short-term measure, say for electoral purposes, they could, of course, increase employment by adding to the number of civil sevants, but to do this would be to flout their whole ethos. Underlying their policy is their conviction that there is no way they can create jobs for people which does not cost the Treasury more than the expenses of maintaining them out of work. This is no doubt true financially; but it leaves out of account the 'social' cost of having people idle. Lord Young attributes the high unemployment figures to an inadequate differential between wages for work and the amount paid out by the state to those without jobs. The solution, he thinks, lies in creating greater incentives to find work, by reducing income tax on those at the bottom of the scale. Incidentally, the Government admit that the overall financial cost of unemployment and supplementary benefit 1986–7 is likely to be £5.6 billion, leaving aside the revenue the Exchequer might have obtained from taxes on income which those unemployed would have earned had they been employed.

I have found widespread indignation in industry about the way the Government allowed the exchange rate of the pound to rocket in the first years of their administration as a consequence of their tight monetary policy, which was designed above all to bring down inflation. This it did, but at the expense of loss of exports and growth in unemployment. Until last year the exchange rate of the pound vis-à-vis the main European currencies was unrealistic in terms of competitiveness.

The Trade Unions

I think it would be the general view of industrialists that the present Government can justifiably claim credit for having reduced the disruptive power of the unions. Sir Peter Carey has put it like this: 'Thanks largely to the policies of Mrs Thatcher's Government, the role of management in industry, which for years had been eroded by the trade unions with the support or acquiescence of governments, has been restored to where it belongs.' Sir John Egan, chairman of Jaguar, believes that in this respect there has been a decided change for the better in manufacturing industry over the past seven years or so: trade union legislation has helped to bring democracy to trade unions and to limit their spoiling powers. The effect of this on the newspaper printing industry is the most recent example of the reduction that has taken place in union power. Of course, the recession has had much to do with it, but the Government are convinced that the secret balloting required by recent legislation has not only limited the number and scale of strikes, but has led to the election of more moderate trade union executives.

While he thinks that there is now more often a common objective between the shop floor and the management in favour of increased output and greater productivity, Sir John Egan believes that British trade union leaders, unlike their counterparts in Western Europe or in the United States, remain uninterested in wealth creation. They see their task as being mainly to promote the terms and conditions of employment of the workforce, rather than to help increase the overall cake from which they will eventually get a larger slice. I put this allegation to the leadership of the labour movement. John Smith MP, the Opposition Spokesman for Trade and Industry, repudiates it vehemently. He believes that the labour movement has faced the challenge of creating wealth as well as of pursuing its traditional search for more equal distribution. For this reason it will give priority to manufacturing industry as the main wealth-creating sector of our society. To try to redistribute wealth on a falling curve of prosperity would, in John Smith's view, be to exacerbate the politics of envy.

Gavin Laird, general secretary of the Amalgamated Engineering Union, also hotly disputes the charge that the unions are not interested in wealth-creation. The main unions involved in the manufacturing sector of the economy are, he says, perfectly aware of the need for good relations between both sides of industry, for wealth-creation as the central objective, and for improved productivity. The unions accept new technology even if it means fewer jobs, provided it helps productivity and hence sales and growth. But he does not think the panacea for better relations lies in legislation or in share-ownership. The clue lies in satisfactory agreements negotiated between the representatives of employers and employees. He instances the agreement concluded between his union and Babcock, a firm whose management had decided that they needed to spend £30 million on investing in new machinery. But they could not justify this investment unless they could be sure of satisfactory relations with the employees. They reached an agreement which provided for a reduction of unit costs for a specific period of time, for a shift system, for the maximum use of the new machinery, and for no demarcation disputes. The whole thing was discussed frankly between the two sides and the agreement was so successful that within three years the management were wanting to make yet another investment of the same scale with a consequent increase in the number of jobs. But, Laird complained, 'we do not normally know what management want'. The biggest failure lies, he is sure, in the lack of communication and in the failure of employers to stimulate middle management or to train and pay them adequately. What in Britain we have to do, Laird insists, is 'to create a climate of identity between management and employees'.

Norman Willis, the general secretary of the TUC, says that in every speech he has made over the last eighteen months he has spoken of the need for wealth-creation. He welcomed Industry Year. On behalf of the TUC he has spoken of the danger that there is not going to be much industry left 'if we cannot generate in our own country a similar sense of common purpose and expertise to that displayed by many of our competitors'. David Lea, assistant general secretary of the TUC, has spoken to me with some pride of the conference he helped to organize last year on 'Innovation'. In his view, and that of most of my interlocutors in the labour movement, it is this need for new ideas and new methods of management that lies at the heart of the matter. Trade unionists and politicians on the left complain that there are too few new products coming along in British industry; and that there are shortcomings in design, delivery and marketing, areas calling for a joint campaign between both sides of industry rather than civil war between them.

That trade union leadership is shifting its ground from defence to attack and accusing management of lack of imagination and drive emerged in my talk with David Lambert. His account of the more aggressive attitude today of the management in their dealings with individual members of the workforce compared with ten years ago was implicit confirmation of the trade unions' loss of clout. Again, he took the offensive on the question of trade union attitudes towards greater output in industry. His union were now prepared to accept Sunday working for the first time. Moreover, he and his union were all in favour of new technology; over the past seven years the labour force in the knitwear industry had been cut by 30 per cent, yet output had fallen by only 10 per cent. Despite existing tension the representatives of employers and employees had a common interest in promoting industrial growth and increased productivity. He was full of praise for the work of NEDO.

Gloomy is the only word that can be used to describe the outlook for this country as seen by John Edmonds. Morale in this country is low; the Falklands War revived it, but it has now slumped again. The sense of national decline is more widespread now than in 1979 because of the high level of unemployment and the absence of any early prospect of large-scale job-creation, particularly in manufacturing industry. The only hope is a change of government. According to Edmonds, would-be investors in manufacturing industry are turned off by the persistent low level of demand in the economy and by the poor quality of our management compared with those of West Germany, the United States and Japan.

Eric Hammond has no illusions about the current performance of British manufacturing industry; but he believes that the ingredients for success are there. Better management is needed and better training of the workforce.

What is essential is that all agreements between the two sides of industry should allow for the following: equal treatment between manual and white-collar staff; the involvement of the workforce in discussions on the performance and prospects of the company; training for people to take on higher-level work, in return for which there would be avoidance of demarcation disputes; and renunciation of industrial action, with reference of unresolved disputes to 'pendulum arbitration'.

Hammond makes an interesting point about recent trade union legislation. He thinks that far from reducing union power, it may well come to have the opposite effect. When it is seen that union executives, having been chosen by the workforce, are fully representative, they will have correspondingly greater authority. As against this, the proportion of the workforce belonging to TUC unions (at present below 40 per cent) is falling, which means a declining *masse de manoeuvre* at their command.

I recall a seminar that took place during my time in Washington between representatives of different areas of the British economy. It was the sort of laundering of our soiled linen that our compatriots like to conduct before the American public, without any inhibition and even with pride. One of the British speakers asked very calmly whether it would not be a good idea if Mrs Thatcher were to resume the previous practice of offering beer and sandwiches at No. 10 to trade union leaders, because this had helped to keep the heat down in industrial disputes. Another British representative rejoined much less calmly that that was exactly what Mrs Thatcher did not intend doing. She felt strongly that trade union leaders had no right to be invited to No. 10 and given privileged access to beer and sandwiches. Indeed, the Prime Minister's view was that it was precisely this kind of attention paid to trade union leaders in the past which had exaggerated their sense of power and encouraged their tendency to behave as though they were a separate estate of the realm.

Management

'*Plus ça change ...*' was the first reaction of Sir John Harvey-Jones, so he told me, on reading again my despatch of 1979. 'You've no idea how bad management has been in this country,' a leading industrialist has said to me. It is a conviction voiced to me frequently by both sides of industry, that the trouble lies in that quarter, with lack of managerial leadership, and one wonders to what extent this has been remedied in recent years and what the underlying causes were, or are, of this national failing. I have nevertheless been encouraged by the widespread view, unsullied by complacency, that in recent years there has been a major change for the better in the outlook and practice of industrial management: more and better people entering industry;

an outlook that is more market-orientated; and greater dedication to technology and training. The shortcomings of training have been another familiar lament from both sides of industry. Lord Young makes no bones about it. According to his figures, '70 per cent of British managers get no training at all during their careers', and they start with 'lower educational qualifications and less training than our international competitors'.

Professor Alan Budd of the London Business School, while admitting the danger of generalizations of this kind, believes that a continuing defect of British management had been their failure to seek with sufficient vigour to expand into new markets; their aim has been to produce at existing levels of output more cheaply by installing labour-saving machinery and cutting the labour force. This has been done with the acquiescence of the labour leadership, those laid off being rewarded with generous redundancies and those retained with pay increases. However, Professor Budd is encouraged by the new-found determination of management to produce more competitively. He also believes that the average worker on the shop floor is more prepared than before to see a connection between output and pay.

Having found one's way to the heart of the maze and been able to hold up management as the main culprit, one is soon told by the managers themselves – for why should they bear all the burden of guilt? – that to blame them is to mistake cause and symptom. Their shortcomings are not their responsibility but are the product of the non-industrial culture to which they are heir; and deeper still, their shortcomings derive from the inadequacies of our educational system as a whole.

Quinton Hazell is another industrialist who deplores this flaw in our educational system. But in discussing the manufacturing problems with me he fastens on another immediate gap: the lack of encouragement for new small businesses employing, say, less than fifteen people. It is essential that these should be granted economic incentives, for example exemption from VAT and rates, as they are in Italy. A small entrepreneur in this country who starts up a business, not using his own money, does not, he points out, enjoy the benefits of the Business Expansion Scheme. This again must be remedied.

From all parts of the political spectrum I have received the particular comment about my 1979 article: that it did not deal with the City of London and its connection with our industrial performance. Sir John Egan is critical of the service provided by the City for the would-be investor in British industry, a system of monitoring and advice that is inferior to that provided in the United States or Japan. John Smith believes that the outlook and structure of the City are 'inimical to manufacturing industry', He sees the City as being interested primarily in investments which produce a quick return. He contrasts this with the practice in West Germany where the banks are closely involved with industry even when they do not hold a large part of the equity.

My own inexpert conclusion on this subject is that the City of London do not regard it as their business to look after industry. As they see it, the prime responsibility of financial institutions is to attend to the immediate interests of their clients, who may well want low risks and high and immediate returns.

Michael Hart, manager of the Foreign and Colonial Investment Trust plc, believes that the City's knowledge of, and contact with, industry has greatly improved over the past decade or so. But, unfortunately, both City analysts and investment managers tend to think short-term: analysts, because the brokers for whom they work naturally want their clients to buy and sell shares; investment managers, because they have to show to directors and trustees adequate performance over regular, often three-monthly, intervals. This emphasis on short-term performance in the City is inevitably felt by industry. Industrialists fear that their share price will fall if they do not produce good profit figures. A takeover-bid may then loom over the horizon. Nevertheless, money is now being raised for long-term projects, e.g. by rights issues, and quite a lot of thought and effort is being devoted to achieving a balance between the needs of long-term investment and the desire for short-term profits.

I have frequently come across the criticism that the policies of the present Government favour the City. Thus high interest rates have meant that wealth accumulates in the City while manufactures decay.

Our Non-industrial Culture and Educational System

Without exception everyone with whom I have spoken places much of the blame for our present economic malaise on our non-industrial culture. For over a century industry has not attracted the best brains and has been a social Cinderella – 'the best natural leaders have not gone to work in industry', to quote a remark I heard countless times. It is almost with a sense of relief, as though it provided a useful alibi, that many of those responsible for industry fasten on this diagnosis.

Sir Alexander Jarratt, who after holding important posts in the Civil Service has had a varied and distinguished career in industry, is worried, as are all the industrialists whom I have consulted, that not enough qualified people are going in to manufacturing industry to ensure its survival. I made enquiries in an attempt to obtain statistical evidence of this and I must say that the outcome is not too discouraging either in trend or in aggregate. On the basis of information provided by the Department of Trade and Industry, the Department of Employment and the Department of Education and Science, out of the total of university graduates who entered employment in 1984 61 per cent went into industry and commerce compared with 57 per cent in 1971. These figures relate only to graduates from universities and do not include graduates from polytechnics. Sir Alexander Jarrratt sees, of course, that the way to increase the proportion of able people going into industry is to raise the remuneration. He believes that rewards in industry have been improving compared with those in other sectors of the economy, except the City, but that on average they are still well below those of our competitors. (According to my information salaries are about 40 per cent higher on average in French industry than in British.) Over the past six or seven years industry itself has been making increased efforts to recruit the right people, to train them and to provide for career management.

In my Valedictory Despatch I did not deal with the general level of education in this country nor with the appropriateness of our system for the requirements of the modern world. So much emphasis has been put on these themes in so many of my interviews that I cannot avoid the issue here.

On the general question of literacy I had hoped to be able to find some figures, rather than have to rely on hearsay and wild surmise. But the Department of Education and Science tell me that they do not collect statistics on this subject which, they say understandably, is bedevilled by problems of definition, measurement and data gathering. Apparently there is no agreed statement on what constitutes illiteracy. An ad-hoc working group has been set up for this purpose by the European Community; I suppose that is a start.

According to a recent National Economic Development Council report called *Competence and Competition*, 50 per cent of the workforce in Britain have a recognized qualification, compared with 66 per cent in West Germany and 78 per cent in the United States.

From cursory enquiries I have made of those teaching at a higher level, I have received an unfavourable impression of the degree of general knowledge of students nowadays applying to enter universities. According to the head of an Oxford college, applicants are now not nearly as well prepared for university entrance as they used to be. They do not, for example, learn or even read poetry. It is suggested that one of the reasons may be the comprehensive system of education, which inevitably puts less emphasis on traditional academic attainment because all abilities and interests have to be catered for. For those framing academic curricula, the future careers of the students have not as a rule been the main gleam in their eye; to be sure, studies and exams along traditional lines, following a pattern pioneered by Dr Arnold, and without any specific end in view – the study of classics is a good example – may still be the most suitable training for many professions. For myself, with little Latin and less Greek, it is with reluctance that I have to admit this. But these humanistic criteria do not necessarily encourage or test qualities such as creativity, design, initiative or organizing skill, which are required for success in industry. No less pertinent, academic curricula and awards may discourage people with other aptitudes who might well, if they pursued different courses of study, qualify for industrial openings.

I was particularly disturbed by the view on the general level of education in this country expressed by Sir James Cleminson, who was recently president of the CBI and is now chairman of the British Overseas Trade Board. He says that the majority of people leaving school at sixteen do not have sufficient education to enable them to assimilate the sort of skills required in modern industry. The root-cause of the deficiency lies in the lack of adequately qualified teachers; a radical shake-up is needed in our education system and in the pattern of remuneration. Cleminson's concern is borne out by comparative research which has been carried out by Professor Sig Prais of the National Institute of Social and Economic Research. He has found that French and German children of average or below-average ability perform much better in simple mathematical tasks than their English counterparts.

This threnody is taken up by Lord Jellicoe, who was Cleminson's predecessor as chairman of the British Overseas Trade Board. 'If we are to arrest our decline,' Lord Jellicoe declares, 'we need to attract to industry a much higher proportion of the country's best brains. And the key to this lies in education.' The same link between education and industry has been drawn by Robert Malpas, managing director of BP. He believes that industry can only prosper 'if the society in which it operates is well educated, with everyone literate, articulate and numerate'. While, therefore, he in no way favours too much stress on specialized education at school age, particularly since it is impossible to guess today what will be required technically tomorrow, he is concerned by the critical shortage of maths and science teachers. 'Two hundred and seventy school physics posts are currently unfilled,' he says, adding that this 'is a crisis requiring emergency solutions'.

The problem with our education system, so Lucy Hodges, the former education correspondent of *The Times*, has explained,

is that it has its roots in pre-industrial Britain. This is not the case with France and Germany, both of which established and developed their education systems in order to revolutionize themselves industrially. Britain had had its industrial revolution by then, and it had happened quite independently of education. Our education system has its roots in the kind of study pursued at the ancient universities of Oxford and Cambridge and at boys' public schools. It was an education for gentlemen, men of leisure, or for those who were going into a particular kind of public service, and it was not for people who were going to get their hands dirty or fiddle about with computers. Thus we have always educated our elite to a high standard, but very narrowly, and we have never developed a proper, comprehensive system of education and training for the population at large.

Sir Geoffrey Chandler, who after a long career in industry has been director-general of NEDO and director of Industry Year 1986, has told me that 'this country is in deep potential crisis'. He believes that this is reversible but only with revolutions in education and in attitudes towards industry. Anything else is merely tackling symptoms, not the disease. The cause of our ills lie in 'an inherited culture and a set of attitudes which put industrial activity at the bottom of the social pecking order and of an education system which, by ignoring or denigrating it, obscures the connection between quality of life and industrial success'. In other words, Sir Geoffrey Chandler believes that if our malaise is to be cured we have to address the fundamental reasons for our decline – our antiquated educational system and our wrong-headed attitude to a career in industry. Gavin Laird offers an identical analysis of the underlying causes of our decline; as for the cure, he believes that, from fourteen years of age, children should be taught something relevant to industry, that teachers should be given experience of industry, and that management should be made to realize that training of their employees is an investment and not simply an overhead cost.

Martin Wiener, in his book *English Culture and the Decline of the Industrial Spirit 1850–1980*, which I mentioned in my introduction, cites Japan to illustrate the connection between the background of culture and economic behaviour. 'No one', he says, 'can fully understand the Japanese economic miracle without grasping the working principles of Japanese culture' – the tribal character of work-relationship and the inner discipline instilled by Japanese upbringing. So I end this section speaking of fundamental causes, rather than symptoms, because I agree that they are at the heart of our dilemma, and because they explain why more time is needed before a verdict can be pronounced on what has been achieved in recent years and a prognosis made about the likely incline of our economy.

Relations with the European Community

In my 1979 Valedictory Despatch I said that our general stance in the European Community (EC) made us seem an uncooperative member, with inevitably adverse results for British economic interests. In areas where we stood to benefit, for example regional development and the social fund, we received fewer rewards than we thought were our due. On matters where we had an excellent case, such as the Common Agricultural Policy (CAP) and the budget, we were listened to with less sympathy than our arguments warranted. And when we stood aside, as in the European Monetary System (EMS), there was a natural tendency for the other members to think of going ahead without us. The impression we gave was that we had joined a club that we did not like and whose rules we wished to change under the threat of leaving if we did not get our way.

To what extent do the other countries in the European Community still view us in the same light? Are we seen as half-hearted members or are we accepted as fully committed?

Since Mrs Thatcher's Government took office there have been a number of factual changes that have affected Britain's relations with the Community. First of all, British exports to the EC countries now amount to 49 per cent of total exports (compared with 33 per cent in 1972). Secondly, Britain has secured a two-thirds reduction in the amount it contributes to the Community budget, thereby solving a problem which dominated relations from our accession to the Community in 1973 until the conclusion of the budget deal in 1984. The Fontainebleau Agreement of 1984 was a turning point. Thirdly, since Britain joined, the Community has been enlarged by the admission of Greece, Spain and Portugal, countries which have brought new problems to the EC. There is indeed a conflict now between the interests of the richer northern countries and those of the southern members of the Community, a clash exacerbated by the fact that France, West Germany and Britain in the northern tier are the only net financial contributors to the Community budget.

These changed features have modified the British attitude to the European Community, as they have our partners' view of us. What was seen by others as the bad example we set in the class has been excelled by that of Greece. However fiercely Mrs Thatcher has battled for 'my money' over the budget she has refrained from threatening to withdraw from the Community. The clear impression I have derived from all the French and Germans with whom I have spoken in politics, government, banking and industry is that they now fully accept Britain's commitment to the European Community. There is no fear that we will pull out or start threatening to do so again unless we get our way. I think that our partners would assume that a successor government in London would be unlikely to reopen the principle of membership, though they see a risk of confrontation with a Labour Government if it ignored the Community's rules on government aid to industry or if it tried to introduce exchange controls or, still worse, import controls.

Not that British public opinion has become enamoured of Europe. Despite the change in the trade pattern and the great increase in British tourism to the Continent, we remain set in our ideas, and the realization that we are now less influential in the world outside has the effect, I believe, of making us more, not less, insular. History, tradition and sentiment all contribute to this; and we are not a people of concepts. I am not sure that I was right in saying in my 1979 despatch that we were pragmatists. I think in fact that we are governed more by prejudice than pragmatism. When we boast of our pragmatism we mean that we are not susceptible to conceptual ideas and that we are not prepared to commit outselves to a principle that may have practical consequences we do not like. To others in Europe we appear more illogical than pragmatic. Take our emphasis on retaining sovereignty even when we have to modify it in practice, as was the case in the recent restructuring of the European steel industry on a Community rather than a national basis, which inevitably involved some infringement of national authority. Take the time-honoured belief of so many of our policy-makers that our particular relations with the United States could not be maintained if we came too close to a more integrated Western Europe, even though the US authorities have been enjoining us to do precisely this and even though it has become evident that our influence in Washington will be in direct ratio to our weight in Europe. Or take an example from domestic politics, the adherence of the Labour Party to the dogma of nationalization long after it has been demonstrated that this was not the best way to run industry or indeed to look after the interests of the mass of the population.

The European Community embodies a major handicap for the British: 65 per cent of the total Community budget goes on agriculture and three-quarters of that 65 per cent on the storage and disposal of surpluses. Yet only 10.7 per cent of the labour force of the Community works on the land – and only 2 per cent in Britain. It is our fault that we were not in the Community from the start to fashion it to suit our industrial interests, rather than those of agriculture; but that does not attenuate present feelings of indignation about the continuing agricultural bias of the Community.

Partly for these reasons, I think, we continue to be regarded, and to see ourselves, as something of an odd-man-out in the European Community despite the recognition of our full commitment. This certainly is the view of Viscount Davignon, who has had as much recent experience of the Community as anyone. He points to the strident way we express ouselves; to our inhibition about wrapping up our intentions in the language of love in contrast with other countries who, when seeking something for themselves out of the European marriage, will harmonize their appeal in a paean of praise for the Community. Of course, it must be recognized that we do rather cultivate a degree of difference between the British and the Continental way of life; and I am not sure that our insular instincts needed the encouragement the Federal German President gave them in a speech in the British Parliament on 2 July 1986, when he implored us to remain as we were. There is a tendency, so I have found, in the Community to see possible advantages for the other countries in our somewhat wayward stance. Thus there is always a hope, which I believe to be exaggerated, that we can exert particular influence in Washington on behalf of Community interests because of our particular relations with the United States and because of our distinctive profile compared with that of the Continental countries.

Davignon believes that censure of the British for their attitude to Western Europe is unfair in present circumstances, given the active and imaginative way London has been trying to promote Community objectives over internal trade, restructuring of traditional industries on a Community-wide basis, technology and the formulation of a common European foreign policy. This favourable view is now held by the French Government, which accepts Britain's commitment to the European Community. The French also believe that the British have given clear evidence of this commitment. The turning point was the 1984 Fontainebleau Agreement on Britain's budgetary contribution. Since then Britain has not merely gone along with the ideas of its partners, but has suggested initiatives and taken practical steps to promote progress. It has done so, for instance, in the field of relations between the European Community and other countries; most notable was the British role in promoting a compromise solution in the agricultural trade dispute between the United States and the EC. Britain has also provided the impetus towards the creation of a genuine internal market in Europe, involving the removal of existing barriers to trade and the liberalization of services, including banking, insurance and other financial services, as well as development of a common transport policy. Nor should one overlook Britain's part in the moves towards closer European integration and long-term sharing of sovereignty by means of amendments and additions to the Treaty of Rome as enshrined in the Single European Act. This new view of Britain's attitude to Europe[4] is helpful over a number of issues where our interests are affected, just as it means there is less evidence of a joint Bonn–Paris relationship in confrontation with London.

The leaders of opinion in the Federal Republic of Germany, political or industrial, would I am sure go along with this. Indeed, they regard us as being in the forefront of those who want to make progress in removing barriers to the creation of a true market in industrial goods and services. The Germans were, I think, amazed by the way we accepted the Single European Act despite its considerable constitutional implications. We are regarded as a partner of growing importance to them; the increase in the number of Mediterranean countries may have had something to do with this, though not so much as the German view of the way Europe is likely to have to develop. According to this, technology, space and defence are the areas in which progress together will have to be made, and Britain must be in the van. Over defence, for instance, it is difficult for the Germans to believe that, looking a generation ahead, the United States will have the same number of

---

[4] The Council of Europe, which has non-political, non-economic objectives in education, culture, human rights and specific fields of administration, for example anti-terrorism, is another European forum in which the British contribution has, I believe, come to be well esteemed.

troops based in West Germany as they have now. Western Europe will have to get its defence act together.

Nevertheless, the Germans see us as 'different' partners, not because of our policy or our attitude to the European Community but because of our individual, even idiosyncratic, approach to many subjects. 'The way to London is longer than to Washington' is how it was put to me by Dr Wilhelm Christians, chairman of the Deutsche Bank, the biggest bank in West Germany. He is struck by the greater rewards and prestige that continue to attach to the City of London compared to British industry, and to the separateness between the two.

Relevant to our value as a European partner is a certain scepticism evident to me in the Federal Republic about our industrial prospects. The decline in our manufacturing industry is something of which the Germans are very much aware, just as they are surprised that we are apparently so insouciant about it. 'What is going to happen when North Sea oil runs out and you have done nothing to utilize the proceeds for reinvigorating British industry and alternative sources of power?' was the sort of question that was put to me on several occasions.

Conclusions

Harold Nicolson described a diplomat as someone who spent his life a stranger in another's country to return and end his days a stranger in his own. Returning to my country after years abroad I do not find myself so much a stranger as a novitiate. The walls of the seminary and the liturgy may remain the same but society is in a state of flux and the mission is no longer guided by the original absolute purpose. Because so many of the externals remain unchanged it is difficult to be certain about what is going on underneath. My career has required me to try to understand and sum up the different countries in which I have lived and to do so rapidly and with a wide sweep. I know no country so difficult to delineate or about which it is so hazardous to generalize as Britain – despite the persistence of traditions and social mores which, in the eyes of many foreign observers, render us so 'different', not to say idiosyncratic. We are, to be sure, a curate's-egg of a country.

Our Janus-like physiognomy is partly responsible for the problem of definition. Martin Wiener has described the cultural polarity which emerged in the last century between Englishness, identified with the pastoral vision ('the green and pleasant land') and industrialization. In this dual context the word 'decline', used so frequently about our present condition, is equivocal.

In one sense, that of manufacturing output, we have been in decline since

1851, the high-water mark of this country's material strength following the first wave of the industrial revolution in the previous century; and Samuel Smiles was expressing the accepted view of the times, the 1860s, in exalting the men who made and manipulated the machinery by which the country had been made great. But to others, affected by the very success of industrialization and its consequences in urban materialism and the dark satanic mills, the country's aims and achievements had to be judged by very different criteria. What mattered to them – to Ruskin, William Morris, Hardy, Chesterton, Belloc, Stanley Baldwin, Arthur Bryant and John Betjeman, to name just a few – were the quality of life (they 'took away' the Englishman's 'maypole'), natural beauty ('our England is a Garden'), rural simplicity ('Merrie England') and a system of education that produced gentlemen fit primarily for the professions. This attitude was not the monopoly of any particular political party. No one, indeed, has summed it up better than J. B. Priestley, a man of the left and an authority on the national character; 'we are instinctively opposed', he wrote, 'to high-pressure industry and salesmanship, wanting something better than a huge material rat race'. After quoting those words, Martin Wiener concludes his book as follows:

> At the end of the day, it may be that Margaret Thatcher will find her most fundamental challenge not in holding down the money supply or inhibiting government spending, or even in fighting the shop stewards, but in changing this frame of mind. English history in the eighties may turn less on traditional political struggles than on a cultural contest between the two faces of the middle class.

Before dealing with the fundamental challenge of the 1980s I must record certain important changes that have occurred and that have brought beneficial practical results. In 1979, judged by the outcome of the election, I think it is fair to say that most people would have regarded the two main preoccupations of the country as inflation and the excessive power of the trade unions. The recollection of the inflation of the first years of Harold Wilson's Government 1974–5 and of the winter of discontent under James Callaghan was decisive in the polling booths. Recognition must now be made of the turnaround in these problems. I also think that account must be taken of a considerable shift in managerial attitudes. These flow partly, but only partly, from the diminished role of the unions. Industry is increasingly ready to provide technical training for teachers, for schoolchildren and for management. Middle management, which holds the key to efficiency, has seized hold of its responsibility for productivity and quality control. But manufacturing industry has to do more to attract enough of the ablest young people, and the Government will have to ensure that more is done to encourage investment in such industry. In my 1979 despatch I deplored the entrepreneurial malaise that had in the 1970s led to the cancellation of two big transport projects – the third London airport and the Channel tunnel; here, again, there has been a change for the better since those days.

Britain is like an old building: you succeed in papering over one lot of cracks only to find fissures appearing elsewhere as a result of faulty or shifting foundations. I cannot say that in her time in office so far Mrs Thatcher has succeeded in changing the frame of mind of the country, although informed opinion is no longer in doubt that, of our two national faces, the anti-industrial one has been too much to the fore for too long. As I said in my 1979 despatch I do not have much sympathy for those who seek to justify our present state of affairs by a pastoral apologia. Those who live in the midlands or the north do not see how they can find salvation in a de-industrialized society. This does not imply a lack of understanding of environmental and conservation movements, or a disregard for the quality of life to be found in many parts of the country. The problem is that Britain has a dense, immobile population. There is no way in which tending sheep, milking cows, cutting corn, catering for tourists, being tellers in a bank or taking in laundry can provide sufficient work for them all, even if they were suited to it.

It will take time, longer probably than Mrs Thatcher originally supposed, to bring about the kind of fundamental shift in outlook that is needed. She may also have come to nourish doubts about the ability of any government to effect sweeping change of this kind. In my 1979 despatch I said that we could reverse the decline if the British people were 'fired with a sense of national will such as others have found these past years'. There is not much sign that this has happened. For war, yes, as the Falklands crisis showed; otherwise one does not gain the impression that there is universal concern about anything being wrong – not surprising, perhaps, given the unchanging nature of many outward features of our national life and the undoubted increase in the standard of living compared with a generation ago. Yet doubts are dawning. I believe that there is a considerable gap between public opinion and that of informed observers. Anybody who has responsibility for any aspect of our economic or industrial affairs is acutely aware of impending doom – unless we take drastic steps. We are threatened with becoming much poorer as a people, compared, say, with the Germans or the French; this, in the not too distant future, is bound to have serious repercussions on many aspects of our national life.

One underlying problem which I did not deal with in my 1979 despatch, and which cannot be overlooked any longer, is our inadequate educational system. I had not by then undergone the cultural shock that affects anyone returning to live in this country after a lengthy absence. It is not a question of which culture you favour, the humanities or the sciences. The danger is that the general degree of education with which people are now leaving school in this country is proving inadequate to equip them for the modern world. It may be asked why this should matter more now than formerly. The answer lies in the increased use by industry of modern technology. Industry nowadays – and business as a whole for that matter – calls for a modicum of knowledge from most of its employees. Our schools are not producing an elite capable of running either government or business, as the French system does; nor do they turn out people adapted to the requirements of engineering or industry, as the German schools do; nor do they provide their students with a good general education at the age of eighteen, as is the Japanese practice. This question of education is a responsibility the Government cannot escape. The solutions and judgements will be long-term. They are not such as to affect immediate votes. There is, however, no graver or more urgent task for any government in Great Britain.

As regards relations with the other countries of the European Community, the last seven years have undoubtedly seen a major improvement. We now know where our economic future belongs, and the other countries accept our commitment. That can bring us, and our European partners, great benefit.

To move on from this to the creation of a truly united Western Europe is a big step, requiring the sort of vision and leadership that nobody at the present time seems to possess in this country or in any of the other countries of Western Europe. Monnet, thou should'st be living at this hour. Would that we could say with confidence that in the foreseeable future there will be a strong unified Western Europe of this kind to which Britain will belong. I am more certain now than ever before that it is only in such a framework that the contradictions of our dual nature can be resolved – the reversal of economic decline set on foot, and the application, for the benefit of others besides ourselves, of the particular qualities that distinguish this country.

BRITAIN'S DECLINE:
ITS CAUSES AND CONSEQUENCES

Text of Valedictory Despatch published by The Economist,
2 June 1979

CONFIDENTIAL   British Embassy
                                                    Paris

The Rt Hon. David Owen MP   31 March 1979
London

Sir – Since Ernest Bevin made his plea a generation ago for more coal to give weight to his foreign policy our economic decline has been such as to sap the foundations of our diplomacy. Conversely, I believe that, during the same period, much of our foreign policy has been such as to contribute to that decline. It is to the interaction of these delicts, spanning my time in the foreign service, that this valedictory despatch is devoted.

The Account of Our Decline

In the immediate aftermath of the war we continued to rank as one of the great powers, admittedly a long way behind the United States and the Soviet Union but nevertheless at the same table as them. A quarter of the world's population did after all still belong to the British Commonwealth and Empire. I myself was able to observe Churchill, Attlee and Bevin dealing on equal terms with Stalin and Truman at the Potsdam conference when no German or Frenchman was present. With the eclipse of Empire, and the emergence of America and Russia, it was inevitable that we would lose comparative power and influence – and to be sure we have been in relative economic decline since the middle of the nineteenth century (when we were still producing two-thirds of the world's energy, and half its iron and cotton cloth and when per capita income in Britain was over twice that in Germany and one-third greater than in France). But in the mid-1950s we were still the strongest European power militarily and economically. We were also well ahead of all Continental countries in the development of atomic energy.

It is our decline since then in relation to our European partners that has been so marked, so that today we are not only no longer a world power, but we are not in the first rank even as a European one. Income per head in Britain is now, for the first time for over 300 years, below that in France. We are scarcely in the same economic league as the Germans or French. We talk of ourselves without shame as being one of the less prosperous countries of Europe. The prognosis for the foreseeable future is discouraging. If present trends continue we shall be overtaken in GDP per head by Italy and Spain well before the end of the century.

A few figures tell the tale of our relative decline:

Table 1 Comparative Growth of GDP Since 1954 (based on figures in US $ at 1970 prices and 1970 exchange rates)

	1954	1960	1977
Britain	100	117	175
France	100	133	297
West Germany	100	164	310

In 1954 French GDP was 22% lower than our own; German GDP was 9% lower. By 1977 French GDP was 34% higher, and German GDP 61% higher than ours.

Table 2 GDP Per Capita (Britain = 100) Since 1954 (based on figures in US $ at 1970 prices and 1970 exchange rates)

	1954	1960	1977
Britain	100	100	100
France	93	103	141
West Germany	93	121	146

Productivity (that is, output per person employed) was about the same in Britain, France and West Germany in 1954, with Britain marginally highest. Table 3 shows how we have fallen behind since then.

Table 3 Growth of Productivity Since 1954 (based on figures in US $ at 1970 prices and 1970 exchange rates)

	1954	1960	1977
Britain	100	116	168
France	100	131	266
West Germany	100	140	277

The exchange rate at any one time may certainly have distorted comparisons of the purchasing power of the pound in relation to the franc and the mark, in the sense that a pound could buy more in London than its equivalent at the prevailing rate of exchange in Paris and Frankfurt, with the result that the index figures for Britain in the above tables may be too low. But the trends, which are based on one price level and constant exchange rates, emerge clearly.

As regards percentage of world trade Britain has likewise declined badly in relation to France and Germany.

Table 4 Share of Manufactured Goods Exported by OECD Countries (percentages at current prices)

	1954	1960	1977
Britain	18.9	15.0	8.5
France	7.2	8.7	8.9
West Germany	12.2	17.4	18.8

I am aware of the efforts made to contest the relevance of these statistics. Many people believe that the lower prices that exist in Britain offset the impact on living standards of relatively inferior wages. But you cannot get away from the fact that a low GDP means a smaller national cake and that there is less wealth to go round. Some will assert that the figures do not represent the true relative strength. Others will argue that the British way of life, with ingenuity and application devoted to leisure rather than to work, is superior to that elsewhere and is in any case what people want. I do not doubt this; nor do I question the agreeableness or quality of life in Britain or the tolerance of the British people. There is depth in our society that others have not achieved. This is inestimable – though it cannot be taken for granted. My purpose is to show how we are faring in relation to others and to suggest the possible effect on our lives of continuing decline.

On the basis of historical experience it seems to me that it would be wrong to assume that a way of life, based as ours is on a relatively favourable and stable economy, will necessarily remain unimpaired if the conditions change. I cannot say that I have much sympathy for those who seek to justify our present state of affairs by a pastoral apologia. They remind me of the French and German nobility of the eighteenth and nineteenth centuries who were against progress, which was synonymous with industrialization. In any case Britain has a large population, accustomed to and skilled in industrial life, who, within the confines of the British Isles, would suffer a sharp drop in standards if they were destined to become the pioneers of a de-industrial revolution.

You only have to move about Western Europe nowadays to realize how poor and unproud the British have become in relation to their neighbours. It shows in the look of our towns, in our airports, in our hospitals and in local amenities; it is painfully apparent in much of our railway system, which until a generation ago was superior to the Continental one. In France, for instance, it is evident in spending on household equipment and in the growth of second homes. But lest these be thought subjective judgements let me give two tables that illustrate what has happened over the past twenty years or so.

Table 5   Average Earnings of Non-managerial Staff in Manufacturing Industry (£ per hour)

	1954	1977
Britain	0.22	1.61
France	0.18	1.92
West Germany	0.15	2.95

Table 6   Registered Private Vehicles (in millions)

	1954	1977
Britain	3.2	14.9
France	2.7	16.5
West Germany	1.4	20.2

Nor do I believe that counter-attack based on our recent reduction in inflation affects the general picture. (This and other retorts are of course required for immediate diplomatic purposes; but that is outside the scope of this despatch.) Such a line of argument begs the question of why we ever allowed inflation to rocket in 1975 to rates far higher than those in France or Germany. Nor does it touch the essential and long-term problem of productivity. Output per man-hour in manufacturing industry (in £ per hour) was as follows in 1977:

Britain	2.70
France	4.50
West Germany	7.10

This is not the place to discuss comprehensively the causes of the poor productivity which epitomizes our decline. The subject is not one of easy solution. But having spent the past seven years in France and the Federal Republic of Germany I have been struck by certain comparisons.

Management

(1) Generalizations on this subject are inevitably unscientific. In many British industries there is no doubt about the high quality of management. But anyone serving abroad soon becomes aware of a lack of professionalism in British management. We have a different attitude towards a career in indus-

try. In the Federal Republic – as indeed in Germany since the time of Bismarck – industry has tended to attract the best people, whereas in Britain those leaving school and university seem less prepared to make a career in industry than to join a merchant bank in the City of London or one of the public services. It is partly a question of tradition and prestige but also one of finance. According to the latest figures, the average salary of a middle-grade manager, adjusted for taxes and differences in cost of living, is nearly twice as high in France and Germany as in Britain.

(2) In France, industry for a long time did not attract the best people, a failure that was partly responsible for France's delayed industrialization. But there has been a remarkable change in outlook in the past quarter of a century and the elite of the country, such as those who graduate from the École Nationale d'Administration, move freely between the top ranks of government and industry. There is a certain parallelism here between France and America. The present French Foreign Minister, Jean François-Poncet, began his career in the Foreign Service and then had a spell in industry before returning to the public service. Or take the new head of Peugeot-Citroen, Jean-Paul Parayre, who at the age of forty-one holds one of the most onerous posts in the country. A graduate of the École Polytechnique, he worked as an official in the Department of Industry before leaving the Civil Service to enter industry. His present salary is over twice that of the chairman of British Leyland, leaving many fringe benefits out of account. The maximum tax on his salary is 60 per cent, whereas that on BL chairman Michael Edwardes's is 83 per cent.

(3) Unfortunately, there is evidence here of the drain upon our engineering and managerial resources produced by the poor relative financial rewards in British industry. Not only are British engineers and managers leaving Britain for overseas French projects but they are coming to work for French and multinational firms in France. For example, one major French engineering firm employs ten British engineers in Paris. It is relevant to record here the great importance the French attach to their famous engineering schools (the Polytechnique and the Ponts et Chaussées, etc.) and to the training of engineers as all-round managers. This opens up for the profession the plums of high industrial command.

(4) So far as the management of major capital projects by government is concerned our vision appears limited and our purpose changeable, at any rate compared with France and Germany. This is particularly noticeable in transport. We started work on two large plans, the third London airport and the Channel tunnel, only to cancel both. To arrive nowadays at London airport from a French or German airport is to be made immediately aware that our standards have slipped.

(5) In trade union structure, as in management, our present difficulties

are rooted in the distant past; they do not arise from recent decisions and cannot be quickly or easily cured.

(6) Neither Germany nor France has craft unions. Membership is based not on occupation but on the industry in which the person works. There is, therefore, no temptation for one craft in an industry to pursue its sectional interests at the expense of another or of the company as a whole. The number of trade unions in the two countries is much smaller than in Britain, as is the proportion of the workforce belonging to them. In Germany there are seventeen industrial unions fully integrated within the DGB (German Trade Union Federation). Since each of these unions would have members among all grades of manual and clerical workers in the plant they would not have conflicting sectional interests. French trade unions are grouped into six major confederations. A major employer in the engineering industry would have to deal with not more than three unions, and each of these unions would claim to represent all workers in the plant. There are 115 trade unions affiliated to the Trades Union Congress in Britain.

(7) These features make it easier in France and Germany to negotiate settlements and to make them stick.

(8) In both Germany and France the closed shop is against the constitution, hence illegal; in both countries collective agreements are binding contracts enforceable in law. In neither country is it the practice for people to go on strike before a wage agreement has expired (in Germany it is illegal to do so). In contrast to Britain, strikers in Germany and France do not receive regular income-tax rebates while they are on strike. Nearly always in Britain in recent years a strike has led to a very favourable settlement for the employees; in France and Germany this has not been so, for example the steel strike in Germany and the air traffic controllers' work-to-rule in France. The Labour Counsellor here cannot think of a single strike in France in the past two years that has achieved its objective.

(9) There is no shop-floor control over production in France as there is in Britain. No French manager thinks twice about changing people's duties or their timetables if that is required for efficiency, nor does he hesitate to install new machinery and instruct people that from Monday onwards they will be working at x instead of y. Neither in France nor Germany has responsibility for production shifted out of the hands of management into those of trade union representatives.

(10) The paradox of the British labour scene at the present time is that, despite the contribution our unions have made towards a better safety record in our factories, their influence and ready resort to strike pressure have not secured better general employment conditions than in France and Germany: not only are real wages lower but hours of work are longer.

(11) In Britain, the proportion of the labour force which belongs to trade

unions is 50 per cent; in France it is 22 per cent, in Germany 44 per cent. The comparison is telling. No less so are the figures set out in Table 7.

Table 7   Days Lost in Industrial Disputes in All Industries and Services (in thousands)

	1957	1977
Britain	6,012	10,142
France	3,506	2,434
West Germany	69	86

Interrelation Between the Economy and Foreign Policy

The bearing of our weakness upon our foreign policy is almost too obvious to require analysis. In the immediate post-war world we were the second most important power in the Far East with all the influence that that carried. We played a major part in the 1954 Geneva conference on Indochina and in the formation of the South-east Asia Treaty Organization the same year. We were the predominant power in the Middle East from Iran to Libya, from Iraq to Aden; we were the only outside power that had troops there, except for the Russians for a short time in northern Iran. The Suez débâcle in 1956 was a sudden eye-opener to the decline of British power in the eastern Mediterranean – as indeed it contributed to it. Our subsequent withdrawal from the Gulf – which, as many predicted, was followed by the loss of Western influence over the price of oil – may have been inevitable at some stage, but it was precipitated by the devaluation crisis of 1967. General de Gaulle was able to say the same year that Britain was too weak economically to be able to join the Common Market.

At the present time, although we still retain certain extra-European responsibilities, for example in Rhodesia and Cyprus, we are unable to influence events in the way we want because we do not have the power or will to do so. It is true that we may have a special relationship with America, and, based as this is upon certain shared traditions and responsibilities, it will continue.

But anyone who has followed American policy towards Europe closely over the past few years will know how much our role as Washington's European partner has declined in relation to that of Germany or France. France, in fact, over a period of nearly two decades pursued a blatantly anti-American policy, but its importance to America is much greater now than at the beginning of that period, because of its economic strength.

As regards Europe, the fact must be faced that for the first time for centuries British policy cannot be based upon the prevention of any single power dominating the Continent because, out of weakness, we would be unable to do this. For more than a decade after 1945 we held back from joining in schemes of greater European unity; we were confident of our superior strength in relation to our European neighbours, and we did not think that anything would succeed without us. Then when the others showed that they were determined to go ahead on their own we found that we were unable to prevent them doing so or to shape what emerged in the way we wanted. For long we underestimated the economic prospects of our European neighbours and for even longer we overestimated our own strength and influence in relation to them.

The recent intensification in the Paris–Bonn relationship owes a good deal to our economic weakness, as to our a-European diplomacy. President Giscard is not really very interested in us at the moment and gives the impression that Anglo-French relations only feature in his mind when the annual summit comes along. It is sometimes said in London that if only we pursued our interests in Europe as ruthlessly as the French did we would have a scoring rate as high as theirs. This is another example of how we overestimate our influence and our nuisance value: we do not count in Europe like the French; the other countries of the Community know that they can get along quite well – some say better – without us as they have done for years. But there is another distinction which I must make in parenthesis here. French policy is certainly hard-headed now, but there is more to it than that: it is constructive about Europe (for example, direct elections, the European Council, the Three Wise Men) which makes the ruthlessness both more effective and more acceptable to the rest of the Community.

I should also interject here that British representatives abroad naturally do their best to prevent too pessimistic a picture of our economy from gaining ground; and, indeed, there are important tasks of correction and proportion to be carried out. But the facts of our decline are two well known for us to be able to persuade foreign observers that there is really little wrong with our industrial scene. Indeed, we harp on our poverty to justify our plea for budgetary changes in the Community. In France we have come nowadays to be identified with malaise as closely as in the old days we were associated with success. In many public statements Britain is mentioned as a model not to follow if economic disaster is to be avoided. It is striking how, at French functions where a British representative is present and there is a need for some obliging observation about us to be made, speakers seem unable to find anything to refer to that has happened since 1940–5, a period which still indeed affords us a good deal of capital. The French press is full of articles about Britain's plight, not least depressing for their patronizing search for favourable elements such as our language and our humour.

We had every Western European Government ready to eat out of our hand in the immediate aftermath of war. For several years our prestige and influence were paramount and we could have stamped Europe as we wished. Jean Monnet and others on the Continent had originally hoped to build a European economic union around the nucleus of a Franco-British union. It was the failure of the British to respond to this idea that led them to explore alternative approaches, in particular the idea of a coal and steel community based upon a Franco-German rather than a Franco-British axis. This was a turning point in post-war history. The French were not very tactful in the way they confronted the British Government with the proposals for the Schuman Plan. But Monnet knew by 1950 that the British Government was not prepared to make the leap necessary to join the sort of organization that he was thinking of, one that would achieve lasting Franco-German reconciliation and set Europe on a new course. He sensed that London did not really believe that the idea would come off, and that in any case their fears of supranationality would deter them. He was correct in his analysis.

But what is amazing looking back is the way in which the British Government reached so important a decision. The full British Cabinet never dealt with the question. Neither the Prime Minister, nor the Foreign Secretary (Bevin was in hospital), nor the Chancellor of the Exchequer, nor the Lord Chancellor, were present at the ministerial meeting which took the decision against British participation in the European Coal and Steel Community (ECSC). At the start of his Foreign Secretaryship, Ernest Bevin was in favour of a European customs union, but this was anathema in the rest of Whitehall, particularly in the Treasury and Board of Trade.

Furthermore, as the centre and right came to power in France and West Germany in the late 1940s, the ideal of a socialist Europe, for which there had been enthusiasm in the Labour Party, looked impracticable. Continental socialists continued to favour progress towards European union and this difference in outlook came to be an important cause of the gap that has existed ever since between them and the Labour Party. In 1950 the National Executive Committee of the Labour Party declared: 'In every respect, except distance, we in Britain are closer to our kinsmen in Australia and New Zealand on the far side of the world than we are to Europe.'

In his maiden speech in the House of Commons, Edward Heath urged the government to join the ECSC. But, despite Winston Churchill's clarion call for a united Europe in the years immediately after the war, the Conservatives when they came to power in the early 1950s did nothing to implement it.

They fought just as shy of supranationality as did the Labour Party. Referring to the ideal of European integration, Anthony Eden said in January 1952, 'This is something which we know, in our bones, we cannot do.... For Britain's story and her interests lie beyond the Continent of Europe. Our thoughts move across the seas....' At the start of the European Coal and Steel Community the *Financial Times* described it as a 'cross between a frustrated cartel and a pipe dream'.

In the mid-1950s we refused to participate in the creation of a European Defence Community, a decision that was largely responsible for its still-birth, and that led as compensation to the formation of the West European Union with the heavy obligation to maintain a specific number of British troops in Germany. It should be emphasized here that this despatch does not attempt to deal with the defence aspects of our policy. We have certainly benefited militarily from close collaboration with the United States; and notwithstanding our economic weakness we have continued to play a highly important defence role in Western Europe, the political implications of which cannot be overestimated.

We withdrew from the Spaak Committee in 1955 which we had been invited to join after the Messina Conference and which had the task of drafting proposals for the creation of a European atomic energy authority and a European common market. We refused to join the former largely because we thought that we would be giving rather than receiving. When we saw that, notwithstanding our absence, and contrary therefore to our expectations, the Common Market was going to come into being we tried to prevent this happening; and when this failed we did our best to encompass it in a free trade area.

This effort, which we described as a 'Grand Design' for Europe, caused considerable resentment on the Continent, where it was looked upon as a wrecking tactic. When it broke down we formed the European Free Trade Association (EFTA), but that was no adequate solution, political or economic. By 1960 the British Government was seeking ways of bringing about a close association with the Six and we then made our application to join the Community, mainly for political – and as so often in post-war British foreign policy, for contradictory political – reasons. We were worried that instability in France and Germany might cause the Community to disintegrate; we were also concerned that if the Community prospered and achieved the promised cohesion it would become something from which we would not want to be excluded, particularly as the United States would be inclined to regard it as its main partner in Europe. When, after de Gaulle's vetoes and further knocking at the door we were eventually admitted to the Community, our policy towards it did not smack of wholehearted commitment even after the overwhelming referendum.

These post-war policy decisions appear to have flowed from a series of questionable judgements. We do not seem to have grasped that relations between France and Germany, the central equation of Europe, were now on a new footing: if not united they were now brought together by the psychological bond of defeat in war – for the first time for nearly a century and a half; the two countries were quits at last and both had a similar purpose in extricating themselves from national humiliation. After 1945 our ethos was quite different, but the foundations of our national life were far from sound. Although we were victorious we were only marginally victorious: we did not have the spur that defeat might have provided, nor did we have the strength with which victory should have endowed us.

Because we had survived the war intact we did not realize fully the motives or strength of the European search for unity. We underestimated the recovery powers of the Continental countries and the great boost that could be given to their industrial development by membership of a common market. We overlooked one of the prime lessons of our own history, that we had been able to spearhead the industrial revolution in the eighteenth century, not because of our size – we only had a third of the population of France – but because, at a time when the countries of the Continent were fragmented by internal tolls and tariff barriers, we were the biggest single market in Europe. We did not perceive fully how the Commonwealth would evolve and the reduced political and economic role that we would have in it. (For instance, we were taken aback when, in 1957, our proposal for a British–Canadian free trade area was turned down by Ottawa.) Continuing for long to believe that we had a unique part to play on the world scene because of our participation in Churchill's three interlocking circles, we were concerned that too close a relationship with Europe would weaken our influence in the other two circles, those of the Commonwealth and America.

There is no doubt that in the years just after the war any loosening of the Commonwealth link would have been inexpedient in the national interest as well as unacceptable to public opinion. Bevin was always saying that he could not choose between Europe and the Commonwealth and, as suggested above, the French were tactless in the way that they advanced the Schuman Plan idea as though it involved a choice of this kind. But in fact at that stage of post-war history to have joined the movement towards greater European unity, of which the Schuman Plan was the first essential step, need not have involved any loosening in the link between London and the other countries of the Commonwealth. By the time the development of Europe would have called for such a reduction in Commonwealth solidarity, the other Commonwealth countries themselves would have been prepared for such a change.

As regards the American connection the paradox has been that from the early days of peace the American Government was promoting the cause of

European unity. Monnet had extremely close contacts in the United States and there is evidence that it was the Americans themselves who stimulated the ideas that led to the Schuman Plan. Yet, as already indicated, one of Britain's hesitations about Europe arose from its fear that participation in plans for greater European integration would lead to a loosening of London's special relationship with Washington.

Finally, and as a reflection of our inability to grasp the importance of the idea of Europe, we persisted in the crucial years of 1955 to 1960 in trying to fit new pictures into old frames. It was almost an obsession with us, at the formative time before and after the Messina Conference, that the Organization of European Economic Co-operation (OEEC) was all that was needed to bring about closer unity in Europe and that no new machinery was necessary. Sir Ivone Kirkpatrick, Permanent Under-Secretary at the Foreign Office, recorded on 25 November 1955 that 'Messina is a doubtful, if not actually wrong approach, and OEEC is a better one.' There was constant concern about overlapping and the wish to avoid untidiness – yet what was at issue was not a matter of efficiency but of politics.

Whatever the reasons behind them, our decisions in these years undoubtedly had an adverse effect upon our economy. We continued for too long to try to play a world role and failed to cut our coat according to our cloth. The Prime Minister was saying as lately as July 1965 that 'our frontiers are on the Himalayas'. In consequence we were overextended financially and then when the realities of our economic weakness became inescapable we had to draw our horns in precipitously. By excluding ourselves from the organization of the Six that drew up the Treaty of Rome we deprived ourselves of the chance of fashioning the organization at the outset to suit our interests.

It is worth bearing in mind that the Messina Conference resolution, the genesis of the Treaty of Rome, made no mention of an agricultural policy – indeed, the word 'agriculture' does not appear in it. Without our presence, the treaty was drafted with the establishment of a common policy in agriculture as one of the objectives of the Community. On the other hand, there was nothing in the treaty that provided for the direction of Community funds to industry.

During the 1960s, the six signatories of the Treaty of Rome were able to develop their trade with each other and to create a large and sophisticated market. We had to content ourselves with continuing to trade in our traditional markets. We missed the opportunity, in the heyday before the rise in oil prices, to intensify our trade with Europe on the scale achieved by the original Six; no less important, British industry did not, at a time when it could have survived and profited by it, have to undergo the disciplines of a single highly competitive market. This has meant that Britain has not paid the same attention as its European partners to the development of high-technology products, or to the application of the latest technology to conventional production.

Twenty years ago we were ahead of France and Germany in many high-technologies; but our leads have been whittled away, perhaps most startlingly in civil nuclear power. There are of course important exceptions and British representatives abroad are continually drawing attention to and promoting our successes. But the French and Germans have tended to go in for meeting a growing demand for equipment that sells on technology, quality and reliability rather than on price. One of our main problems at the present time, which flows directly from the absence of adequate competitive pressure in the key years of the 1960s and early 1970s, is that our age-long tradition of producing goods of high quality has been impaired. We are unable to match the formidable quality-control standards set by Continental manufacturers, for example in the production of automotive components.

We have indeed gone so far down market that we now tend to become subcontractors where we do not get the benefits of high added value. (The British manufacturing industry, may it be said in parenthesis, has also found itself unable to meet the demands of the hard-headed British consumers, who have increasingly looked to foreign producers.) The half-heartedness of Britain's political commitment to Europe is reflected in a similar lack of total involvement by British industrialists in meeting the requirements of the highly competitive Continental market.

World economic conditions have been particularly difficult during the years that we have been a member of the Community. The Community itself has been under severe strain and has been searching about for means of increasing its cohesion in the face of a world outside becoming colder and colder. The policies we have pursued towards it, or rather the style of our diplomacy, have not been a contribution to this task. Renegotiation distracted the European community for nearly eighteen months from what should have been its prime task of coping with the oil-price crisis; not did it do anything substantial to correct the financial problems of our membership.

It is impossible to say with any precision how much membership of the Community could have helped us if our commitment to it had been more wholehearted. Our entry coincided with a world recession which we, largely as a result of our own earlier policies, were less able to withstand than our new partners. But there is no doubt that our general stance in the Community has made us look an uncooperative member, with inevitable results. In areas where we should stand to benefit, for example, regional development and the social fund, the rewards for Britain have been less than we hoped. On points where we have an excellent case, such as the CAP and the budget, we are listened to with less sympathy than our arguments deserve. And when we stand aside, as in the EMS, there is a natural tendency for the other eight to think in terms of going ahead without us.

The Future

Even the most pessimistic account of our decline contains grounds for hope. The fact that France and the Federal Republic of Germany have managed to achieve such progress in so relatively short a time shows what can be done if there is the necessary will and leadership. Anybody who remembers the state of affairs in those countries in the decade following the war and compares it with the present day must conclude that nothing in a country's future is inevitable and that everything depends upon the national purpose. So far as we are concerned, if the fault that we are underlings lies 'not in our stars but in ourselves', we are surely capable, unless our national character has undergone some profound metamorphosis, of resuming mastery of our fate. But a considerable jolt is going to be needed if a lasting attenuation of civic purpose and courage is to be averted. North Sea oil should provide the material impulse, just as coal did two centuries ago. There are human elements that favour us compared with others: our political stability and the absence of that tendency to explosion that could always afflict France.

It would be outside the scope of this Valedictory Despatch to try to chart the course that we might follow to turn round our present situation. Obviously there are no simple solutions and the difficulties are to be found as much in attitudes as in institutions. At the risk of oversimplification I should like to end with three conclusions based on the years I have spent at the end of my career in France and Germany and comparing their present situation with ours.

First, if we are to defend our interests in Europe there must be a change in the style of our policy towards it. This does not mean giving things up or failing to assert our rights and requirements. It does mean, however, behaving as though we were fully and irrevocably committed to Europe. We should be able to put at the service of the Community the imagination, tolerance and common sense that have formed our own national institutions. We could have ideas to contribute. Pragmatism may be a good basis for the government of a more or less uniform country speaking a single language, or for the conduct of foreign policy from strength when the aim is simply to prevent another power dominating Europe, but it may not be a panacea for creating something quite new and ambitious in international affairs, an organization embracing different peoples of varying languages and traditions. This may call for the sort of originality of political thought in foreign affairs that we contributed in earlier times to the theory of government.

There is certainly an acute problem ahead over our net budgetary contribution to the Community. We have been hardly done by here. We are not going to find an easy solution whatever we do. So far as money is concerned the Community is imbued with a spirit of grasp and take. But there is only one way to go about it if we are to hope to get our way, and that is to have a heart-to-heart talk with the leaders of the other eight countries on the basis that we are an unreserved and constant member interested in the fortunes of the Community as a whole. To issue a warning of withdrawal if we do not get our way would not help our Community partners believe that we would have more to lose than they by our withdrawal.

Secondly, viewed from abroad, it looks as though the facts of our present circumstances are not universally recognized in Britain. The British people do not give the impression that they are fully aware of how far Britain's economy has fallen behind that of our European neighbours or of the consequences of this upon living standards. Naturally people are conscious that they are better off now than twenty-five years ago but they may not know to what extent others in Europe have done much better or of the efforts needed to reverse the trend. As Isaac Newton wrote, the important thing is 'to learn not to teach'. It may be our turn to learn from others, having been teachers for so long.

In this fact-facing exercise the authorities may have a role to play so as to ensure that the public do not remain in ignorance of something that is a matter of national concern. It is impossible for anyone of my generation to forget how little the British Government of the 1930s did to enlighten the British people about the rise of Nazi Germany. The needs today are certainly of a different kind but there does seem to be a responsibility upon government to prevent people being unaware of something that will certainly one day affect their future. There is also a task of explaining the Community to the British public rather than making it the scapegoat for our ills.

Finally, and as a corollary to this process of enlightenment, there would appear to be a need at the present time to do something to stimulate a sense of national purpose, of something akin to what has inspired the French and Germans over the past twenty-five years. No doubt the sort of patriotic language and flag waving of former times is inappropriate for us today. The revival of Germany has not owed anything to that kind of stimulus. But nevertheless the Germans have felt motivated by the dire need to rise from the ashes in 1945, and they have had to recover from their past politically too. Hence the dogged devotion to democracy that the Germans have shown since the war and the obligation that every one of them feels to make a contribution to economic, as well as political, recovery. Reaching out from their traditional Bismarckian policy of trying to balance East and West, the Germans have now identified their cause with commitment to the West.

The French on the other hand have found their national revival in a more traditional appeal to patriotism. They started at the bottom of the pit but it has not only been de Gaulle who has played on the need to overcome the country's sense of defeat and national humiliation. Giscard is no less ready to play on chauvinistic chords. In a speech that he made recently which lasted only eight minutes he used the word 'France' twenty-three times and the word 'win' seven times. Yet, to those who have known the French people in earlier days, it is impossible to believe that they are necessarily readier to make sacrifices or to respond to patriotic appeals than their British counterparts.

These then are the words with which I would like to end my official career, and if it is said that they go beyond the limits of an Ambassador's normal responsibilities I would say that the fulfilment of these responsibilities is not possible in Western Europe in the present uncertain state of our economy and of our European policy.

A representative abroad has a duty to draw the attention of the authorities at home to the realities of how we look, just as he has an obligation to try to persuade the government and people of the country to which he is accredited that present difficulties must be kept in perspective. The tailored reporting from Berlin in the late 1930s and the encouragement it gave to the policy of appeasement is a study in scarlet for every post-war diplomat. Viewed from the Continent our standing at the present time is low. But this is not for the first time in our history, and we can recover if the facts are known and faced and if the British people can be fired with a sense of national will such as others have found these past years. For the benefit of ourselves and of Europe let us then show the adaptability that has been the hallmark of our history – and do so now so that the warnings of this despatch may before long sound no more ominous than the recorded alarms of a wartime siren.

Index

Afghanistan, 73, 77–8
Aldington Report (on Balance of Trade in Manufactures), 120–1
Anglo-French Executive Committee (Channel tunnel), 32
Anglo-French Financing Group, 8–9, 32
Anglo-French Study Group, 8
Anglo-French Treaty, 1986 (Canterbury), 63
Argentina: invades Falklands, 80, 85–7; Haig's attitude to, 86, 89; British demand withdrawal from Falklands, 88–90; US arms deliveries suspended, 89, 93; demands, 90, 92–3; sovereignty, 90; disbelieves British readiness to fight, 91; behaviour of junta, 92, 107; Britain warns of intention to attack, 94; and Peruvian peace plan, 95, 99; military forces and actions, 96–9; avoidance of humiliation, 99–100, 103–6; declines British proposals, 100–1; threatens to break relations with USA, 102; and Haig's proposals for Falklands administration, 105; surrender, 106; intransigence, 106
Arias Stella, Dr Javier, 98
Armstrong, Sir Robert, 62, 111
Arnold, Dr Thomas, 131
Auroux, Jean, 10, 13, 51, 55, 59–60, 63

Babcock Company, 126
Bahr, Egon, 71
Baker, Kenneth, 39
Baldwin, Stanley, 138
Bank of England: *Quarterly Bulletin*, 119
Basic Treaty, 1972 (Germany), 69
Bayne, Nicholas, 111
Belaunde Terry, Fernando, 98
Belgrano see *General Belgrano*
Belloc, Hilaire, 138
Betjeman, Sir John, 138
Bevin, Ernest, 143, 151, 153
Biffen, John, 19–20
Bismarck, Prince Otto von, 69
Bonn/Paris Conventions (1955), 70
Boublil, Alain, 25, 28, 41–2
Bouygues, Corinne, 41
Bouygues, Francis: Henderson visits, 26–8; at Paris press launch, 41; denounces Euroroute, 42; in Britain, 54; and Parayre, 55; and Expressway, 57–8
Brandt, Willy, 68, 71
Brazil: and Falklands dispute, 100, 102–3, 105
Britain: government interest in Channel tunnel, 10–11; commitment to German reunification, 70; and French-German reconciliation, 71, 153; insularity, 72; French attitude to, 74–5; relations with European Community, 75, 133–7, 140, 150–7; in Falklands War, 85–7, 91–3, 101–4; US support for in

Index

Britain—*cont.*
    Falklands, 93; proposals to UN on Falklands, 100; and US role in Falklands, 107; economic statistics, 113–20, 144; manufacture and service industries in, 120–1; government detachment from industry, 121–2; investment overseas, 124–5; education and culture, 130–3, 138–40; industrial decline, 137–40, 143–58; national frame of mind, 138–9; quality of life in, 145; decline as foreign power, 149–50; admitted to EEC, 152; and high technology, 154–5

British Rail: on Channel tunnel traffic, 46

Brittan, Samuel, 119, 124

Broackes, Sir Nigel: heads Euroroute group, 11, 14, 27; proposes merger with CTG, 19; rivalry with, 35; financing of scheme, 35; presents film to press, 40; restricts advertising, 41; meets Ridley, 45; lunches with Henderson, 50; and tunnel mandate, 52, 56; and Sherwood, 54, 59; invites Henderson to meeting, 55; criticizes Ridley, 59; *see also* Euroroute

Bryant, Sir Arthur, 138
Budd, Alan, 112, 129
Bullard, Sir Julian, 111
Burns, Sir Terence, 111
Bush, George, 78
Business Expansion Scheme, 122, 129
Butler, Sir Michael, 111

Callaghan, Ian, 18
Callaghan, James, 138
Canada: proposed free-trade area with Britain, 153
capital formation, fixed, 119
car ownership, 117, 146
Carey, Sir Peter, 111, 122, 125

Carli, Guido, 119
Carter, Jimmy, 77–8, 80
Chadeau, André, 20
Chandler, Sir Geoffrey, 111, 133
Channel, English: fixed link, 7–8, 20; proposed bridge, 40
Channel tunnel: opposition to, 7–8, 20; drive-through proposals, 8–9, 14, 21–2, 24, 52, 54, 58; guidelines ('An Invitation to Promoters'), 22–3; trade advantages, 25; traffic and revenue forecasts, 33–4; local environmental consequences, 39; proposed public enquiry, 39–40
Channel Tunnel Group (CTG): formed, 8–9; approaches the Government, 9–10; Henderson chairs, 11, 13–14; seeks French partner, 12, 26–9; composition, 14–17, 64; faith in project, 17; summary of scheme, 21–2; financing, 27, 32–6, 38; public relations, 27, 55; signs agreement with France Manche, 32; Board disagreements, 32; executive committee, 32; operation of tunnel, 36; internal disputes, 36–7; on scale of traffic, 38, 60; and local (Kent) considerations, 40; written submission, 43–6; estimated traffic, 46–7; meets assessment teams, 50; reconsiders drive-through, 52, 54, 59, 62; rejects merger with Euroroute, 53–4; awarded mandate, 61–2; merges with France Manche, 63; incorporated, 64

Charrin, Hervé, 29
Cheriton (Kent), 39
Chernobyl, 73
Chesterton, G. K., 138
Chetwood, Cliff J., 15, 19, 53, 64
Chevalier, Jean-Marie, 119
Child, Denis M., 16, 53, 64
Christians, Wilhelm, 112, 137
Churchill, Sir Winston S., 106, 151, 153

Index

City of London: and industry, 129–30, 137, 147
Clark, William, 100–1, 105
Clarke, Kenneth, 112, 116
Clemenceau, Georges, 70
Cleminson, Sir James, 111, 132
Common Agricultural Policy (CAP), 133, 155
Commonwealth, British: and European Community, 153
Competence and Competition (NEDC report), 131
Conqueror, HMS (submarine), 94–5
Conservative Party: and European idea, 151–2
consumer prices, 115
Costa Mendez, Nicanor, 92, 93, 98
Council of Europe, 136n
Cozens, Mary, 30
Cuba: Bay of Pigs landing, 77

Dalyell, Tam, 94–5
Davignon, Vicomte Etienne, 112, 135–6
Deflassieux, Jean, 27–8
detente, 70–1, 73
Dick, Alistair, 34
Ditchley Park: 1968 conference, 68
Dominican Republic, 77
Dover Harbour Board, 41
Drogheda, Garrett Moore, 11th Earl of, 112
Dunwoody, Gwynneth, 22

Eagleburger, Larry, 100
earnings and wages, 116, 131, 143, 145–7
Eban, Abba, 80
Economist, The, 2, 111
Eden, (Sir) Anthony (*later* 1st Earl of Avon), 152
Edmonds, John, 112, 123–4, 127
education: and British industrial performance, 130–3, 138–40
Edwardes, Sir Michael, 147
Egan, Sir John, 111, 125–6, 129

Ehmke, Horst, 112–13
El Salvador, 77
Eliot, T. S.: *The Cocktail Party*, 37
Enders, Thomas, 87, 89, 99, 106
European Coal and Steel Community (ECSC), 151–2
European Community (EC): British attitude to, 75; and Britain's economic performance, 111; Britain's relations with, 133–7, 140, 150–7; enlarged, 134; agricultural bias, 135; founded, 152, 154
European Defence Community, 152
European Ferries, 48–9
European Free Trade Association (EFTA), 152
European Monetary System (EMS), 133, 155
Euroroute (consortium): formed, 9, 10 & n; scheme, 11, 23–4; proposes merger with CTG, 19; and French cooperation, 25–6; financing, 33, 35; as rival to CTG, 35, 40, 42, 51; Mitterrand favours, 62
Eurotunnel: formed from CTG and France Manche, 63
exchange rate (sterling), 125, 144
exports: of manufactured goods, 116
Expressway, 45, 47–8, 52–5, 57–8, 62

Fabius, Laurent, 23
Falkland Islands: British task force in, 80, 90–1; invaded by Argentina, 80, 85–7; US interest in, 85; Britain insists on Argentine withdrawal, 88, 90; search for diplomatic solution, 90–1; sovereignty, 90, 101; exclusion zone, 94, 96; British land in, 101–4; Haig's framework agreement on administration, 104–5
Fawcett, Sir James, 111
Fieldhouse, Admiral John, 91
Figueiredo, General João Baptista de Oliveira, 100, 102
Financial Times, 14, 35, 152

Index

Flexilink, 41, 53
Fontainebleau Agreement (1984), 134, 136
France: desires Channel link, 7, 42; timetable on Channel link, 10–12; CTG seeks partners in, 12, 26–9; favours drive-through tunnel, 21; and financing of tunnel, 33; press launch of scheme, 41–2; approach to foreign policy, 67, 71–5; commitment to German reunification, 70; reconciliation with W. Germany, 71, 75, 153; sense of global mission, 71–3; attitude to Britain, 74–5; economic statistics, 113–20, 144; and British commitment to Europe, 134, 136; economic revival, 147, 156–7; trade unions in, 148–9; relations with USA, 149–50; European policy, 150; and high technology, 155
France Manche, 32, 46, 50, 52, 54, 63
François-Poncet, Jean André, 112, 147
Franklin, John, 17, 64
Freeman, Richard, 111
French Revolution, 72–3
Fretwell, Sir John, 20, 111

Galtieri, General Leopoldo Fortunato, 88–9, 98
Gaulle, Charles de, 72, 149, 152, 157
General Belgrano (Argentine warship), 93–9, 108
Germany, East (German Democratic Republic), 69
Germany, West (Federal Republic of Germany): approach to foreign policy, 67–72; and reunification of Germany, 68–70; decentralization and diversity in, 69; membership of NATO, 69; defence, 70; French reconciliation with, 71, 75, 153; lacks sense of national mission, 72; economic statistics, 113–20, 144; industrial co-determination, 123; finance and industry, 129; and British commitment to Europe, 134, 136–7; US troops in, 136–7; trade unions, 148–9; and high technology, 155; economic recovery, 156–7
Gibb, Frank R., 15, 37, 64
Giersch, Herbert, 119
Giscard d'Estaing, Valéry, 71–2, 74, 150, 157
Glamorgan, HMS (cruiser), 97
Gorbachev, Mikhail, 69, 77
Gordon, General Charles George, 80
Gordon, Michael, 17–18, 33, 38
Greece: in European Community, 134
Grenada, 77, 79, 85
Gross Domestic Product, 113–14, 116, 118–20, 143–4
growth (economic), 120
Guest, Melville, 18, 37, 44, 59
Gueterbock, Tony, 12–13, 15, 38–40
Guigou, Elisabeth, 25, 112

Haig, Alexander: and Falklands diplomacy, 78, 81, 86, 88–108; relations and meetings with Pym, 88, 94–5, 97, 103–4, 106; meets Mrs Thatcher, 90; and Peruvian plan, 97–8; and sinking of *Belgrano*, 98–9; requests cessation of military action, 99; and British proposals, 100–2; and Latin America, 102–4; and proposed cease-fire, 104; framework on administration of Falklands, 104; with Reagan in Europe, 105–6; effect of role in Falklands dispute, 107–8
Hammond, Eric, 112, 123, 127–8
Hannay, Sir David, 111
Hardy, Thomas, 138
Hart, Michael, 111, 130
Harvey-Jones, Sir John, 111, 121, 128
Hastings, Max, 93
Hayes, Sir Brian, 112
Hazell, Quinton, 111, 129

Index

Heath, Edward, 151
Hemingway, Martin, 47
Henderson, Sir Nicholas: chairs CTG, 11, 13–14, 32; signs agreement with French partners, 31–2; receives CTG salary, 37; hands over to Pennock, 63; and sinking of *Belgrano*, 94, 97; 1979 Valedictory Despatch, 111, 122, 131, 133, 139 (text, 143–58)
Hermes, HMS (carrier), 97
Heseltine, Michael, 38
Hessig, Jean-Jacques, 29
Hitachi Electronics company, 123
Hodges, Lucy, 112, 132
Holland, Don A., 15–16, 64
Honecker, Erich, 69
Howe, Sir Geoffrey, 14, 25, 59
Hunt, Don, 15, 38
Hybrid Bill (on Channel tunnel), 20, 39, 42

Independence, Declaration of (USA), 76
industrial relations, 148–9; *see also* trade unions
inflation, 120, 125, 138
Intermediate-range Nuclear Force (INF), 79
International Maritime Organization (IMO), 11, 26
Iran: US hostages in, 88
Israel: invades Lebanon (1982), 106

Japan: trade dominance, 81; labour costs, 116; industrial achievements, 122–4; cultural background, 133
Jarratt, Sir Alexander, 111, 130–1
Jellicoe, George Patrick John Rushmore, 2nd Earl, 112, 121, 132
Jenkins, Roy, 112, 121
Jenkins, Simon, 93
John of Gaunt, 7
Joint Venture Agreement (CTG/France Manche contractors), 32

Kaletsky, Anatole, 112
Kennedy, Edward, 87
Keswick, John Chippendale Lindley ('Chips'), 14
Keynes, John Maynard, Baron, 77
Khomeini, Ayatollah, 77
Khrushchev, Nikita S., 2
Kirkpatrick, Sir Ivone, 154
Kirkpatrick, Jeane, 87, 100–1
Kissinger, Henry, 78
Kohl, Helmut, 69, 71

labour costs, 115–16
Labour Party (British), 134–5, 151–2
labour relations *see* industrial relations
Laird, Gavin, 112, 126–7, 133
Lambert, David, 112, 123, 127
Latin America: and Falklands dispute, 85, 89, 92–3, 98, 102–3, 105
Layton, Michael John, 2nd Baron, 40, 45
Lea, David, 112, 127
Lebanon, 106
Libya: US air attack on, 80, 82
Liesner, Thelma: *Economic Statistics 1900–1983*, 118–19
Lille, 55–62
Lincoln, Abraham, 76
Louis XIV, King of France, 73
Lundgren, Nils, 119
Lyall, Andrew, 12, 38, 59

McDowall, A., 64
McGregor, Sir Ian, 11
Malpas, Robert, 111, 132
management: British weakness in, 127, 128–9, 138, 146–8
Manhattan Project, 79
Mannesmann (company), 70
manufacturing industry: in Britain, 120–1
Marshall Plan, 76, 78
Mast, Hans, 119
Messina Conference (1955), 152, 154
Midland Bank, 16, 64

163

Index

Mitterrand, François: and Channel tunnel, 10, 60–3; and Third World, 72
Monde, Le, 73
Monnet, Jean, 75, 140, 151, 154
Monroe, James, 85
Montagner, Philippe, 29
Moore, Christopher, 17, 64
Morris, Fiona, 37
Morris, Quentin, 18, 28–9, 32, 34
Morris, William, 138
Moynihan, Patrick, 87

National Westminster Bank, 16, 64
National Economic Development Council (NEDC), 127, 133
National Economic Development Office (NEDO), 127, 133
New York Times, 102
Newton, Sir Isaac, 157
Nicaragua, 77
Nicholas, Herbert: *The Nature of American Politics*, 77
Nicolson, Sir Harold, 137
North Atlantic Treaty Organization (NATO), 69–70, 78
North Sea oil, 117, 137, 156
Nott, Sir John, 2n
Noulton, John, 39

O'Neill, Tip, 87
Organization of American States (OAS; Rio Treaty), 89, 92–3, 98, 102, 104
Organization of European Economic Cooperation (OEEC), 154
Osborne, Alan, 16, 64
Ostpolitik, 68, 71
Owen, David, 38

Parayre, Jean-Paul: accompanies Bouygues, 26; Henderson visits in Paris, 28–9; in London, 30–2, 35, 51, 55; and language problem, 42; and submission of Channel scheme, 42; Henderson meets at Stansted, 42–3; accepts drive-through idea, 52; and mandate, 53, 55; and SNCF agreement, 60; signs concession agreement, 63; position and earnings, 147
Parkinson, Cecil, 112
Parliament (British): and Channel tunnel, 49–50
Parsons, Sir Anthony, 97, 100
Paterson, I., 64
Paye, Jean-Claude, 112
Pennock, Raymond, Baron, 63
Perez de Cuellar, Javier, 97, 104
Peru: seven-point plan for Falklands, 95–9; as intermediary, 100
Poland, 67, 73
Port Stanley (Falklands), 94, 106
Potsdam Conference, 143
pound sterling: exchange rate, 125, 144
Prais, Sig, 132
Priestley, J. B., 138
productivity, 114, 144, 146
Pym, Francis, 24; negotiates over Falklands, 88–9, 92–5, 97, 100, 103–4, 106; and sinking of *Belgrano*, 95

Quilès, Paul, 10, 25–6, 28

rabies, 20, 50
Rainbow Warrior (ship), 41, 73
Reagan, Ronald: on USSR, 76–7; lifts grain embargo on USSR, 78; and US need for allies, 79; statement on foreign policy, 80; suspends nuclear negotiations, 81; on Falklands, 85–6; supports British action in Falklands, 95, 103; telephones Mrs Thatcher, 100–1, 105; visits Europe, 105–6
Rees, Peter, 9
Reeve, John, 31, 64
Reid, Sir Bob, 19
Renault, Jean, 29, 60
Renwick, Robin, 112

Index

Ridley, Nicholas, 9–10, 22, 45–55, 57–61, 63
Rohwedder, Detlev, 113
Rome, Treaty of, 154; *see also* European Community
Roosevelt, Franklin D., 76
Royal Navy: and Falklands War, 91
Rudeau, Raoul, 12
Ruhfus, Jürgen, 113
Ruskin, John, 138
Rutherford, Malcolm, 49n

San Carlos (Falklands), 103
Sarmet, Marcel, 28–9
Schlesinger, Arthur, 76
Schmidt, Helmut, 67–8, 70–1
Schröder, Gerhard, 68
Schuman, Robert, 75; plan, 151, 153–4
Sealink, 10, 49
Select Committee for Transport (House of Commons): Report (1981), 8
service industry, 120–1
Shakespeare, Bill, 15, 57
Shakespeare, William, 8n
Sheffield, HMS (cruiser), 85, 91
Sherwood, James, 10, 45–9, 51–4, 56, 59
Shultz, George, 81
Single European Act, 136
Smiles, Samuel, 138
Smith, John, 38, 112, 126, 129
Société Nationale des Chemins de Fer Français (SNCF), 20, 46–7, 60
South Georgia, 91–2
Spaak, Paul-Henri: Committee (1955), 152
Stannard, Colin, 15, 60
Stansby, John, 55
Stansted airport, 42–3
Star Wars, 13, 79
state visits, 74
Steel, David, 38
Sterling, Sir Jeffrey, 35
Stoessel, Walter, 100–1, 106
Strauss, Franz Josef, 68
strikes, 148–9
Suez crisis (1956), 81, 86, 108, 149
Suffolk Street (London), 18
Sunday Times Insight Team, 93
Sweden, 123

Tacitus, 80
Tarmac (construction company), 9, 64
Taylor, Robert, 112
taxation, 117, 125
Tebbit, Norman, 23
technology, 154–5
Thatcher, Margaret: and Channel tunnel, 7–8, 10, 13–14, 23–5; on Star Wars, 13; relations with Reid, 19; French doubts on, 21, 42; Henderson meets, 24–5, 51; Lille meeting with Mitterrand, 54–5, 60–2; signs tunnel treaty, 63; on US lifting of grain embargo, 78; and Falklands War, 80, 90; and US air attack on Libya, 82; and sinking of *Belgrano*, 93–4; Reagan telephones on Falklands, 100–1, 105; meets Reagan, 106; and British economy, 111, 117; treatment of trade unions, 128; and British EC budget contributions, 134; and national frame of mind, 138–9
Thiolon, Bernard, 20–1
Time magazine, 119
Times, The, 23, 35, 59, 93
Timms, Kate, 13, 112
Toshiba company, 123
tourism, 121
trade unions: power, 125–6, 128, 138; and wealth creation, 126–8; conservatism and diversity, 147–9
Trades Union Congress (TUC), 127–8
Train de Grande Vitesse (TGV), 13
Transport, Department of (British), 11, 16, 45, 60
Triangle House, Hammersmith, 14–15, 18
Truman, Harry S., 80

Index

unemployment, 115–16, 120, 124–5
Union of Soviet Socialist Republics: relations with East Germany, 69; opposes German reunification, 69–70; pipe-line agreement with, 73; US conviction of wickedness, 76–9; as threat to Europe, 81; and Falklands dispute, 90, 105–6
United Nations: and Falklands dispute, 89, 93, 100–1, 104, 106
United States of America: approach to foreign policy, 67, 75–82; commitment to German reunification, 70; French attitude to, 74; attitude to USSR, 76–9; belief in solutions, 78–80; air attack on Libya, 80, 82; either/or-ism, 81; attitude to Europe and Britain, 81; and Latin America, 85, 102–3, 105; concern over Falklands War, 85–6, 100, 107–8; support for Britain in Falklands, 93, 101, 108; Argentina threatens to break relations with, 102; concern for effect of defeat on Argentina, 106–7; labour costs, 115; industrial management in, 123; British relations with, 135, 149, 154; agricultural trade dispute with European Community, 136; troops in Germany, 136–7; attitude to European Community, 152–4

Veinticinco de Mayo (Argentine warship), 96
Versailles Summit (1892), 106
Vietnam, 78

wage rates *see* earnings and wages
Wallace, C. W., 98
Washington Post, 106
Washington, George, 76
Waterloo station (London), 28
Weinberger, Caspar, 2
Weizsäcker, Richard, 67–8
Wellington, Arthur Valerian Wellesley, 8th Duke of, 50
West European Union, 152
White, John, 111, 124
Wiener, Martin: *English Culture and the Decline of the Industrial Spirit 1850–1980*, 3, 133, 137–8
Williams, D. P., 19
Willis, Norman, 112, 127
Wilson, Harold, 138
Wilson, Woodrow, 76
Woodman, Christopher, 39
Woodward, Admiral Sir John (Sandy), 90, 96
Wyatt, Terrell, 53, 64

Young of Graffham, David Ivor, Baron, 23, 112, 122, 125, 129